AF429479

KEYS TO EFFECTIVE SEDUCTION

ILLUSTRATED SAYINGS TO CONQUER AND NURTURE LOVE

ARTURO JOSE SANCHEZ HERNANDEZ

2024

CONTENTS

PREFACE

"Keys to Effective Seduction: Illustrated Sayings to Conquer and Nurture Love" is an essential work for anyone looking to improve their courtship skills and strengthen their romantic relationships. By combining the wisdom of traditional sayings with the innovation of AI-generated images, this book offers a unique and enriching experience.

In this book, you'll discover how to overcome irrational thoughts that can hinder the courtship process and learn to interpret sexual signals effectively. It delves into the qualities needed to spark sexual interest and maintain a healthy romantic relationship, highlighting the importance of both verbal and non-verbal communication.

This edition introduces AI-generated images that humorously and intricately illustrate the sayings, providing a modern and visually appealing complement to traditional wisdom.

It also includes a collection of Cuban compliments and witty remarks that add a touch of humor and authenticity to the courtship process. Additionally, you'll find practical advice presented through sayings and maxims, guiding you every step of the way to win the heart of your beloved.

"Keys to Effective Seduction" not only provides you with the tools necessary to win over that special someone but also helps you nurture and maintain a long-lasting and fulfilling relationship. This book is your ideal companion on the journey of love, blending tradition and modernity to offer you a comprehensive and accessible guide.

Dr. Arturo José Sánchez Hernández.

The Author

～～

INTRODUCTION

If there's one topic that seems to be in no man's land, it's courtship. It's not officially taught in any institution, as if it were assumed that it's something extraordinarily simple that anyone already knows or can spontaneously learn. However, the reality is that romantic pursuit leaves many unresolved questions for a lot of people, and for some, especially during adolescence, it can be truly unsettling.

This book aims to address some of those questions by reflecting on the key moral qualities necessary for effective courtship.

Courtship can be defined as the set of behaviors, unique to each species, used to sexually attract a partner, which allows for the establishment and maintenance of a loving bond. These behaviors make it possible to adequately satisfy many of the needs that arise in a romantic relationship.

Those who struggle with courtship may find it difficult to meet many of these needs, or they may do so inadequately or insufficiently, which can significantly affect their quality of life.[1]

Positive moral qualities, on the other hand, are personality traits that enable appropriate self-regulation of behavior and adaptive relationships with oneself, others, and the world around us.[2] These qualities are expressed in mature and effective ways of thinking, feeling, and acting, in the sense that they bring about the best outcomes not only for the individual who thinks, feels, and acts but also for those affected by their actions. One area of life that demands not only effectiveness but also maturity is courtship and sexuality.

Since courtship projects one's personality in a holistic manner and tests many social skills, the moral qualities necessary for effective courtship are also crucial for an individual's success in many other areas of life—not just erotic or sexual domains—and are essential for adapting well in social settings.

The subject of courtship concerns anyone who wishes to find a partner, or who already has one and wants to maintain a quality relationship, which includes the majority of human beings. The moral qualities discussed here are important for everyone. Considering the number of people interested and affected, as well as its significance in each individual's life, it can rightly be said that this is an important topic that deserves proper research and dissemination efforts.

Throughout history, there has been a wealth of literature addressing courtship or related topics. The Bible, particularly in the books of Proverbs and Ecclesiasticus, offers abundant exhortations and advice on the qualities to seek in a woman and how to treat them according to their characteristics.

In India, Vishnu Sarma wrote the Panchatantra around 200 BCE, which delves into the theme of man's vulnerability to feminine charms.[3] In the same country, Vatsyayana, whose life is thought to have spanned between the 1st and 6th centuries CE, wrote the Kamasutra, a work that illustrates how to enjoy an already established relationship, how to court more effectively, and whom to court.[4]

The Roman poet Ovid (43 BCE - 17 CE), in his *Art of Love* (*Ars Amandi*), offers advice on where to find women, how to court and win them over, how to maintain or rekindle their love, and how to prevent others from stealing it away.[5]

Among modern writers who have gained popularity on the topic, one can cite the German philosopher Erich Fromm (1900 - 1980) with *The Art of Loving*, a work in which he asserts that love is an art that requires knowledge and effort and is the answer to the problem of human existence. He also explores the nature of love in its various forms and its significance in society.[6]

Masters, Johnson, and Kolodny, in *Human Sexuality*, a text that could be considered a classic in the field of sexuality studies, dedicate a chapter to intimacy. They present rules for effective communication, discuss psychological obstacles that hinder the achievement of a satisfying romantic relationship, and emphasize the importance of listening, non-verbal language, anger management, and maintaining expressions of affection toward one's sexual partner.[7]

Currently, there are many texts on this subject, including Bible of Seduction by Alex Hilgert,[8] Practical Manual of Seduction Masters by Mario Luna,[9] How to Master the Art of Seduction Safely and Naturally by Arturo Andrade,[10] The World's Greatest Lovers by Margaret Nicholas,[11] among many others. Each of these works has its own merits but is crafted according to the peculiarities of the authors' societies and cultures.

In Cuba, journalist and Master of Science in Sexual and Reproductive Health, Aloyma Ravelo, in her book *Sex, Love, and Eroticism: Words that Provoke*, dedicates a chapter to the art of seduction. She explores topics such as the importance of courtship for mutual understanding between partners and for determining whether the other person is truly what one seeks, the behavior of courtship in different eras and cultures, the neurotransmitters involved in falling in love, the origins and manifestations of jealousy, and the communicative resources necessary to maintain a high-quality romantic relationship.[12] She has also published articles on courtship in serial publications like the magazines *Somos Jóvenes* and *Mujeres*, as well as in the newspaper *Juventud Rebelde*.

Despite the abundance of literature on the subject, the author of this research believes there is a significant shortage of texts that approach it from a Cuban cultural identity perspective. Moreover, the author has not found any works on this topic that focus on the theory of values. In this research, both universal and authentically Cuban elements are considered, with a reflection on courtship through moral qualities, which constitutes its main novelty.

Another unique aspect is the structure of the work itself, which, based on theoretical arguments about the analyzed qualities, integrates resources such as sayings, proverbs, maxims, images, and glossaries of terms. These elements complement each other, enhancing the reader's understanding of the topic at hand.[13]

Lastly, another innovative feature is the promotion of moral qualities by leveraging the appeal of the courtship theme, especially during adolescence.

Given that the possible circumstances in which someone might try to sexually attract another person are practically infinite, the number of moral qualities that would be needed is vast. This book is not a treatise on morality, but there is a group of these qualities that, due to their importance, cannot be overlooked.

In this work, these qualities are divided into four groups: The first group highlights prudence as a necessary quality for appropriately choosing whom to court and rejecting what is not suitable. The second group includes qualities needed to detect and interpret the sexual signals a woman emits and to understand what we are feeling in that relationship. These include perceptiveness, discernment, objectivity, introspection, and the ability to empathize with others' perspectives.[14]

The third group consists of qualities that enable effective interaction with others, particularly with women. These include civility and its components: courtesy, tact, flattery, generosity, discretion, decorum, self-confidence, and a sense of humor. The fourth group focuses on the qualities necessary for self-control: boldness, patience, promptness, perseverance, equanimity, and resignation.

A central position assumed in the treatment of the mentioned moral qualities is that of the "golden mean," according to which these qualities occupy an intermediate position between vicious extremes—one due to deficiency and the other due to excess or distortion.[15] This concept is wisely expressed in the Latin phrase: *In medio stat virtus* (Virtue stands in the middle).[16]

This approach allows for the presentation of effective ways of thinking, feeling, and acting, as well as their possible deviations. Regarding the importance of showing both the correct and incorrect paths, José Martí remarked in his notions on logic: "To know how we will succeed, it is useful to know in which cases and in what ways it is possible to err."[17] He continues by explaining: "When giving someone directions on the path they should take, we should not only tell them the paths they should follow, but also the ones they should avoid."[18]

For each analyzed quality, its definition and vicious extremes are provided, along with related sayings or proverbs, and images that graphically represent a proverb or saying.

It should be noted that proverbs, sayings, or maxims that are sometimes quite similar have been used. This is not out of fear of not being understood, since each group is preceded by an explanation, but rather to allow the reader to choose the one that best suits their lexicon and way of reasoning.

Additionally, the images not only make the interaction with the text more enjoyable but also facilitate the understanding of the content. Both the images and the sayings, proverbs, maxims, and preceding explanations complement each other, together forming guiding and inspiring systems of reflection.

This work aims to delve deeper into the study of courtship through a reflection on moral qualities, from the perspective of Cuban schools of psychiatry and value theory. It primarily addresses the following questions: What is courtship? How does one court? What are the best and worst conditions for courtship? Why is it important to choose the right person to court? What ways of thinking, feeling, and acting make courtship effective, and which ones hinder it? What should be done in the case of unrequited love? Does courtship end once a relationship is established? What role should sexuality and courtship play in our lives?

The text consists of an introduction, six chapters, general advice on courtship, a compilation of Cuban compliments and witty remarks on romantic conquest, and a glossary system with the most important terms used in the work.

In the first chapter, the foundational concepts are presented. In addition to defining what courtship is, it clarifies what constitutes effective courtship and what does not. The importance of both verbal and non-verbal communication during courtship is discussed, as well as the most common irrational thoughts that hinder the ability to attract a partner from a sexual perspective.

The second chapter addresses the skill of properly choosing or rejecting whom to court, and it reflects on the quality of the criteria for selection and exclusion. The third chapter explores the qualities that enable one to detect and interpret a woman's sexual signals and our feelings toward her.

The fourth chapter reflects on the qualities necessary for effectively interacting with others, especially with women, while the fifth chapter focuses on those qualities that make adequate self-control possible.

In the sixth chapter, the relationships between the analyzed moral qualities are discussed, and recommendations are made for post-conquest behavior. Finally, there is a call to responsibility regarding courtship and sexuality in general.

The general advice on courtship provides an overview of the main ideas presented in the work. These ideas are concisely stated, briefly explained, and concluded with a maxim, proverb, or saying.

For this study, a systematic review of works by authors such as Vatsyayana,[19] Ovid,[20] Erich Fromm,[21] Alex Hilgert, Mario Luna, Arturo Andrade, and others was conducted. Classical authors in ethics like Aristotle, Plato, Seneca, and Socrates, as well as recent researchers in the field of value theory such as the Argentine philosopher and anthropologist Risieri Frondizi, the Cuban philosopher José Ramón Fabelo Corzo, and the Cuban psychologist Fernando González Rey, were also consulted. In the field of psychiatry, there is significant influence from the Cuban psychiatrist Alberto Clavijo Portieles.

Regarding the maxims, proverbs, and sayings, a systematic review of texts like the Bible, the Tao Te Ching, the Analects of Confucius, encyclopedias, and dictionaries of famous quotes and sayings was conducted, as well as the works of José Martí and the researcher Samuel Feijóo. The author also collected those heard from the everyday speech of Cubans in his daily life.

For those sources where the author, country of origin, or book of origin could be identified, this information has been placed in parentheses at the end of each one.

The images in this latest edition were created using the DALL-E 3 artificial intelligence from Chat GPT Plus, tailored to the objectives of the work, with the guiding principle of reaching the reader's heart in the simplest way possible.

The work has been enriched from a practical perspective with interviews and focus groups involving people of different ages and both sexes,[22] as well as with the experience the author has gained, first working with adolescents as a family doctor and later in the psychiatric and sexuality consultations he has been conducting for years.

Despite the diversity of sources and the relative complexity of the text, it is written in simple and direct language, making it easy to understand for those who read it.

One of its limitations is that many of its arguments are valid only for the author's time and culture. However, this is not a significant flaw, as the book is aimed at an audience that shares these aspects.

This work can contribute to the development of courses with an ethical-axiological and psychiatric-sexological profile, to raising the general culture of the population through the dissemination of its results, and to meeting the growing and urgent demand for literature on the theory of ethical-moral values.

It is primarily intended for male adolescents, although it can be useful to anyone who needs to engage in courtship, regardless of age or gender. Additionally, women might find the male perspective on romantic conquest interesting.

The book compiles guiding and inspiring reflections, making it a useful self-help resource for readers and an auxiliary text for those practicing psychotherapy, especially in the field of sexuality.

It offers answers to many questions that can arise at any age but are common during adolescence, making it also useful as a supplementary text for those who work with this age group.

The text addresses moral qualities of extraordinary relevance for proper social functioning, making it a valuable reference material for professionals who foster these qualities in their work: family doctors, psychologists, psychiatrists, educators, re-educators in penitentiary centers, etc. It can also be useful to researchers and those interested in the subject matter.

Having presented the reader with the historical background on the topic, the positions and sources used in the creation of the work, as well as its novelties, limitations, intended audience, and potential beneficiaries, it is now fully at your disposal for consideration.

~~~

Chapter 1: SOME NECESSARY CLARIFICATIONS

This chapter defines what constitutes effective courtship and what does not. It explores the importance of communication in romantic pursuits and analyzes the best and worst circumstances for falling in love. Finally, it debunks irrational ideas that inhibit or paralyze this process.

What Is and What Isn't Effective Courtship?

Effective courtship means knowing how to attract a partner sexually, using an appropriate approach that allows both individuals to navigate the necessary path towards a romantic relationship. But it's not about attracting just anyone indiscriminately; the key to success in romantic pursuits lies in distinguishing between potential partners who are worth courting and those who are not.

It also doesn't mean doing whatever it takes to sexually attract a particular woman. Effective courtship includes the ability to recognize when we don't stand a chance with someone and knowing when to redirect our efforts toward someone else.

Furthermore, it's not about mastering an infallible technique that ensures every woman we're interested in falls madly in love with us. Knowing how to court effectively increases the chances of success, but even the most experienced don't always achieve a romantic relationship with every attempt.

Communication and Courtship

To sexually attract a woman, she must be receptive to our charms, which means courtship is not a one-way street. It's a process of mutual understanding and closeness, where emotional and physical harmony is progressively achieved, while neutralizing the fear, distrust, and aggression that this approach can generate.

How do we achieve this mutual understanding and closeness, and this emotional and physical harmony? Through communication.

– Communication strengthens the chain of love.

– We love what we know. (Or what we believe we know)

Communication is the process of conveying or exchanging information, ideas, or attitudes. It occurs not only through the meaning of spoken or written words but also through non-verbal forms, such as the tone and inflection of voice, speaking speed, silences, personal appearance, body language, gestures or gifts, and the environment chosen to communicate something.[23]

He Who Knows How to Listen, Knows How to Speak. (Egypt)[24]

But what should be communicated to sexually attract a woman? What should be said or expressed? Essentially, you win her over by showing or hinting at romantic intentions and by resonating with her. This is achieved by listening to her, asking questions about topics that interest her, encouraging her to talk about herself, and discussing what interests her rather than what interests you.[25]

– Two good ears often dry up a hundred tongues. (Benjamin Franklin)[26]

By doing this, you'll communicate that, in time, you'll be a good lover who knows how to attend to her needs, including her sexual needs. On the other hand, if you speak selfishly about what interests you, without considering what interests her, you'll be communicating selfishness, showing that you'll only think about yourself and your satisfaction.

– He who talks too much cannot listen. (Panama)[27]

It's important to note that non-verbal language largely escapes the conscious control of the individual, revealing their inner world without them realizing it. Nevertheless, as much as possible, we should pay attention to the non-verbal elements of communication during courtship.

A Good Appearance Is a Letter of Recommendation and
Credibility. (Spain)[28]

You should pay attention to your image and personal appearance. Although physical condition isn't everything, it's an important part of sexual attraction. Additionally, women often associate, consciously or unconsciously, the care of our outward appearance with the quality of our inner world and our ability to meet their personal tastes and the needs of a future family.

–*Good appearance and good manners open important doors. (Spain)[29]*

–*A well-dressed devil is taken for an angel. (Spain)[30]*

–*As they see you, so they will treat you.*

–*As They See the Suit, So They Treat the Servant. (Spain)[31]*

It's also important to ensure that there is consistency between our words and our non-verbal cues. For example, if you are showing genuine interest in her, while listening, you should look deeply into her eyes, avoiding distractions from what's happening around you.

On the other hand, the tone and inflection of your voice, the speed of your speech, or your body language can indicate insecurity, which is usually poorly received by women, who almost always reject an insecure man.[32]

–*A timid love is held in low regard.*

–*A timid love is soon replaced.*

The Best and Worst Circumstances for Courtship

The Best Circumstances for Courtship Are Those That Favor Communication

The best circumstances for courtship are those that facilitate communication, mutual understanding, and emotional connection. It's important that both individuals feel comfortable and relaxed in the environment, with no distractions that could disrupt the process of getting to know each other. This means creating a setting where the temperature, smells, and sounds are pleasant, and where there's a sufficient level of privacy.

However, these ideal circumstances aren't always available. Often, opportunities arise that aren't perfect, but they're still worth taking advantage of. There's also a big difference between a romantic dinner, where you can create an atmosphere like the one described, and the initial approach to a woman, where it's enough to have conditions that allow for a minimum level of privacy and communication. In fact, waiting for perfect circumstances to make a move is often just an excuse for shyness.

– Looking for the Best Often Means Missing Out on the Good. (Spain)[33]

– The Best Is the Enemy of the Good. (Spain)[34]

On the other hand, there are circumstances that are very unsuitable for courtship, not only because the environment makes communication difficult or impossible but also because they are unpleasant and cause significant discomfort.

– In barren soil, a seed does not sprout.

Groups and Courtship

Due to the internal dynamics of groups and the pressure they exert on their members, both men and women often feel watched and uncomfortable when courting or being courted in that context. This discomfort hinders mutual closeness, so it's advisable to separate the lady from the group.

–Divide and conquer.

–Separate to dominate.

If it's not possible to separate from the group, actions taken within it should be concealed from its members.

–It is a great fault to reveal what should be hidden.

–Discretion is one of the secrets to success.

Discretion in this regard is very useful, as secrecy adds mystery and excitement to the romantic pursuit, becoming a great incentive. Moreover, by being discreet, you can avoid the jealousy of those who may try to protect the lady from the supposed bad intentions of the suitor. Discretion also guards against obstacles that might arise from potential competitors, who often appear when intentions are made public too soon.

It's important to clarify that the goal is to avoid the inhibiting influence of groups, not to make enemies of each of their members. Generally, it's beneficial to win the favor of the lady's friends, companions, and family members, especially those closest to her.

Places Where Courtship Happens Most Frequently

Since attracting someone sexually requires communication, the places where courtship happens most frequently are those that offer the greatest opportunities to interact with the lady, such as school, work, or any other place where both of you regularly spend time.

If the woman who has caught your attention doesn't frequent the same places as you, communication isn't guaranteed. Therefore, it's important to establish ways to reconnect with her, such as getting her phone number, email, social media contacts, or information about where she studies or works.

The Importance of the Places Where Courtship Happens

If You're Looking for Fish, Don't Climb a Tree. (China)[35]

One thing to consider is that the characteristics of the places you frequent will determine the types of women you'll encounter there. Therefore, the type of woman you want as a partner should guide the places you choose to frequent.

–To catch fish, go to the river. (Spain)[36]

–To hunt, you have to go to the forest.

Positioning yourself in the right place increases the chances of contact and communication with women who possess the qualities you desire, which in turn increases the likelihood of starting a romantic relationship with one of them.

–With the right conditions in place, in the right setting, and using the right technique, something is bound to happen.

–He who walks among honey will end up getting sticky. (Colombia)[37]

On the other hand, there are places frequented by women with qualities you may want to avoid. If you also frequent these places and maintain contact and communication with them, the chances of starting a relationship with undesirable aspects increase.

–He who walks with filth ends up stinking.

–He who plays with fire sooner or later gets burned. (Afro-Cuban saying)[38]

IRRATIONAL THOUGHTS THAT HINDER COURTSHIP

There are thoughts that result from a distorted reflection of reality and inappropriate generalizations, which inhibit or paralyze an individual when trying to sexually attract another person. Among these are:

"Women only pay attention to very handsome men."

There's Always a Love That Weeps. (Cuba)[39]

It's very common to see beautiful women with unattractive men, which leads to the conclusion that you don't have to be an Adonis to attract and win a lady's love. No matter how far you are from cultural standards of beauty, there will always be someone who sighs and loses sleep over you.

– *The luck of the ugly, the handsome desires.*

– *The heart has reasons that reason does not understand.*

"Women only pay attention to men with great financial prospects."

When There Are No Dogs, You Hunt with Cats.

It's not necessary to be wealthy to have a partner. Financial prospects aren't the only factor women consider when choosing or rejecting a man, so it's wise to focus on moving forward with the resources and possibilities you have at the moment of romantic pursuit, rather than wasting energy lamenting what you don't have.

– *Focus on what you have and what's available, not on what's missing.*

– *When what works isn't available, what doesn't work will do. (Argentina)[40]*

– *Everyone chews with the teeth they have.*

– *Do what you can, with what you have, where you are. (Theodore Roosevelt)[41]*

"Women always have complete control over themselves and the situations in which courtship takes place."

Women, like men, are also full of insecurities and paralyzing attitudes, even the most beautiful ones.

– *When it comes to love, anyone can lose their composure.*

"There are men with a hundred percent success rate in their romantic pursuits."

Playing and Losing, It Can Happen. (Spain)[42]

You may have been listening to talkers who, in a dramatic and exaggerated manner, only speak about their conquests and not their failures.[43] Even in almost ideal conditions and with extensive experience in courting, no one is successful all the time.

–*Playing and never losing—that just can't be. (Spain)[44]*

"I must succeed in all my courtship attempts, as failure in a romantic endeavor is a disgrace."

No one is obligated to succeed all the time. Unless you're ashamed of your human condition, there's no reason to be embarrassed by something that happens fairly often.

–*The one who advances the most is the one who walks and falls, but gets back up, rather than the one who doesn't move for fear of falling.*

–*Don't miss out on the joys of life for fear of failure.*

–*The issue isn't hitting the target, but launching the arrow; the issue is not being afraid of life.*

Additionally, being rejected by one woman doesn't mean you'll be rejected by all.

–*What one woman doesn't want, another begs for. (Spain)[45]*

–*What some detest, others desire.*

"Beautiful or successful women are too difficult. They're not for me."

A Cowardly Man Doesn't Enter the Palace.

Many men are afraid to pursue a very beautiful or successful woman. They think she must have a very handsome boyfriend, an exceptional lover with great financial prospects, who gives her attention they could never remotely offer. Based on this belief, they are convinced they have no chance.

The reality is that very beautiful women are often quite lonely because no one dares to court them. Sometimes they exercise and follow diets thinking that improving their physical appearance will solve their loneliness, but by becoming more attractive, they generate even more fear and attract even fewer suitors.

Because of this, the chances for those who dare, using the right technique, can be quite high. Contrary to what many believe, the more beautiful they are, the more opportunities you might have.

–*Fear is conquered by daring.*

–*He who doesn't risk, doesn't cross the sea. (Spain)*[46]

–*Glory is conquered by storming it. (José Martí)*[47]

–*Nothing has been written about cowards. (Afro-Cuban saying)*[48]

FINAL CONSIDERATIONS

Up to this point in the analysis, several important clarifications have been presented. Generally speaking, the following can be stated:

- Effective courtship means attracting a partner sexually, but not just anyone, and not a specific person at any cost. Being effective in courtship includes the ability to distinguish between potential partners who are worth pursuing and those who are not, as well as recognizing when you have no chance with someone and need to step back.

- Communication is of paramount importance during courtship, to the extent that the best circumstances for romance are those that favor communication, while the worst are those that hinder or block it.

- For emotional and physical harmony—essential in courtship—to develop, it's necessary to communicate or subtly convey romantic intentions, both verbally and non-verbally, and to ask about and discuss topics that interest the woman rather than focusing on your own interests.

- There are thoughts, resulting from a distorted reflection of reality and inappropriate generalizations, that can inhibit or paralyze an individual when trying to sexually attract another person. It's important to avoid these.

Having presented these elements, which might be considered introductory, we are now ready to move on to the qualities necessary for high-quality, effective courtship, among which those related to making the right choice of whom to court play an important role.

~~

Chapter 2. CHOOSING WHOM TO COURT

This chapter reflects on the importance of making the right choice and the criteria to do so.

The effectiveness and quality of courtship begin with the ability to distinguish between people who, due to their qualities, are desirable and suitable to be courted and those who are not—this is essentially prudence.

> *−Prudence is the ability to distinguish between things that can be desired and those that should be avoided. (Cicero)[49]*

Some reasons to make a good choice include:

What starts as a game can gain strength

Look before you leap. (England)[50]

Many relationships that start as a simple game end up becoming stable and long-lasting. Therefore, it is wise to consider whether that relationship would be beneficial if it were to solidify.

> *−Measure twice, cut once.*

> *−Don't test the depth of the water with both feet.*

> *−Neither marry without seeing nor sign without reading. (Spain)[51]*

> *−Before you marry, be sure of what you're doing. (Spain)[52]*

Both bring about changes in each other

Love makes equals of those who love each other.

When you start living with another person, both of you undergo transformations, and each one takes on qualities of the other.

–You take on the shape of the stick you lean on. (Cuba)[53]

–Love makes equals of those who are not.

–Two who sleep on the same mattress soon share the same opinion. (Spain)[54]

–If the rose joins the onion, it soon smells like scallions. (Puerto Rico)[55]

–A woman will change even the way you walk. (Spain)[56]

Therefore, with a good choice, you are likely to adopt good habits; while with a poor choice, the opposite may occur.

–Bad company corrupts good manners.

–A rotten apple spoils the bunch. (Spain)[57]

–With the saints, you'll be a saint; with the lost, you'll be lost. (Mexico)[58]

Both influence each other's life projects

A low-quality relationship filled with dissatisfaction and worries will negatively impact many areas of life and prevent the emotional stability needed to aim for higher goals and pursue them until they are achieved. Additionally, the habits acquired with your partner can either benefit or hinder your life projects.

–A man often marries a woman to be made; hence the torments. (José Martí)[59]

–With a good woman, an empty house becomes full. (Spain)[60]

The qualities of the woman significantly impact the upbringing of children

Whose children you want, whose woman you have.

No matter how profound a man's knowledge of education is, a woman's role in raising children is irreplaceable, and her personal qualities are of extraordinary importance in this regard.[61]

−A woman's worth is reflected in her children and her home. (Spain)[62]

Compatibility of character is essential for the emotional stability of both

I prefer to live with a lion or a dragon than to live with an evil woman. (Ecclesiasticus 25:16)[63]

If there's no compatibility of character with your partner, or if they have an uncontrollable bad temper, how could the home possibly be a haven of peace or a refuge from life's struggles?

- *Better to live on the edge of a roof than in a spacious mansion with a quarrelsome woman. (Proverbs 21:9)[64]*

- *Better to live in the desert than with an irritable and quarrelsome woman. (Proverbs 21:19)[65]*

- *A quarrelsome wife is like a constant dripping on a rainy day. Trying to stop her is like trying to stop the wind or hold oil in your hand. (Proverbs 27:15)[66]*

- *A contentious woman, a hateful woman. (Spain)[67]*

It's important to note that these proverbs and sayings have been crafted from a male perspective, but the ideas proposed are equally valid when considering the impact of a man's bad temper on a woman and the couple's relationship in general.

- *Smoke and a bad attitude drive people out of the house. (San Salvador)[68]*

- *By offending and mistreating others, we end up alone.*

- *Those who sow offenses reap loneliness.*

The behavior of a partner can be a source of great distress

He who has a bad woman by his side is always on edge. (Spain)[69]

Life already has enough complications without also having to worry about a partner's behavior.

− *From love that does not suit, many ills and few goods arise. (Spain)[70]*

− *The discontented spouse always lives in torment. (Cuba)[71]*

− *There is no heavier burden than a wayward woman. (Spain)[72]*

Regarding disorganized and reckless behavior in sex, it's worth noting that in our macho culture, such behavior is often tolerated and even encouraged in men while being condemned in women. However, these behaviors, whether in men or women, can cause significant distress in the other partner and severely damage the romantic bond.

− *Some seek in the square what they have in abundance at home. (Spain)[73]*

− *Many go looking elsewhere for what they already have at their doorstep. (Spain)[74]*

− *Consider if what you're searching for is worth what you're losing.*

− *He who doesn't care for what he has is prone to lose it. (Afro-Cuban saying)[75]*

The lazy woman leaves everything for tomorrow. (Spain)[76]

There are many other vices and disorganized behaviors, not directly related to sex, that are extremely harmful to the couple and the family. These include addictions, extravagant and wasteful financial behavior leading to difficulties or the inability to manage the household, laziness, lack of hygiene, among many others.

−A woman with vices is a woman to despise.

−A thoughtless woman is a bad pantry.

−The woman who turns to wine, to what other vices will she not turn? (Spain)[77]

Many more arguments could be cited, but those mentioned are enough to underline the importance of choosing wisely whom to court and knowing when to reject what is not suitable.

−Seek the good woman and avoid the bad. (Spain)[78]

CRITERIA FOR SELECTION AND EXCLUSION

Even the Best Wood Has Some Ants

When it comes to choosing whom to court and rejecting what is not suitable, it's essential that the criteria for selection and exclusion are of high quality. Therefore, reflecting on these criteria is necessary.

The answer to how these criteria should be is very personal, as qualities considered very good and desirable by some may not be so for others, without either being wrong.[79]

– *There's no accounting for taste. (Spain)*[80]

– *What some detest, others desire. (Spain)*[81]

– *What one person rejects, another begs for. (Spain)*[82]

Whoever Loves the Rose Doesn't Mind the Thorn[83]

On the other hand, if the criteria are extraordinarily high, it's possible that no woman in the world will meet them. This, instead of helping, will prevent finding a partner since all will be excluded.

–*He who looks for a flawless wife remains unmarried. (Romania)*[84]

–*Even the best wood has some ants. (African saying)*[85]

–*There's no woman or mule without blemish.*

–*Every mule limps on its leg. (Cuba)*[86]

–*There are no roses without thorns. (Spain)*[87]

–*There's no forest without dry branches. (Romania)*[88]

–*There's no sky without clouds, nor paradise without snakes.*

The reality is that we ourselves have plenty of flaws, so it's not about finding a perfect woman but one whose imperfections harmonize with our own.

–*Each to their own. (Spain)*[89]

–*Every sheep with its mate. (Spain)*[90]

–*Two who love each other should resemble each other. (Mexico)*[91]

–*Each one for each, Pascuala for Pascual.*

Scabies gladly does not sting and if it stings it does not mortify. (Cuba)[92]

There may be a situation where a woman possesses qualities so valued by us that it feels worth enduring significant flaws. In such cases, one must weigh the criteria for choosing and excluding.

–*He who dies by his own choice finds even the earth welcoming. (Panama)*[93]

–*He who willingly becomes an ox licks the yoke. (Mexico)*[94]

–*He who dies by his own choice finds death sweet. (Cuba)*[95]

–*If you die by your own choice, may death taste like coconut candy. (Cuba)*[96]

‐ *To each their own taste. (Mexico)*[97]

Love that doesn't suit, may it not be mine.

While overly high standards in choosing a romantic partner can be an obstacle to finding one, lacking standards or having flawed ones can lead to relationships that later cause many problems that could have been avoided.

–*He who eats both good and bad eats double, but might get indigestion.*

–*Some seek refuge in a beehive. (Malaysia)[98]*

–*Love that doesn't suit brings many troubles and few benefits. (Spain)[99]*

–*Those who marry for looks alone often pay a steep price. (Chile)[100]*

–*The roses fall, but the thorns remain. (Argentina)[101]*

FINAL CONSIDERATIONS

One thing that should never be taken lightly is the choice of whom to pursue romantically. In this regard, it can be said that:

- The effectiveness of courtship begins with knowing whom to choose and whom to reject, making the quality of selection and exclusion criteria very important.

- There are many reasons to carefully choose whom to court, such as: what starts as a game can grow stronger, both individuals influence each other and their life projects, the woman's qualities greatly impact the upbringing of children, compatibility of character is crucial for the emotional stability of both, and the behavior of our partner can be a significant source of distress.

- If the selection and exclusion criteria are extraordinarily high, it might be impossible to find a woman in the world who meets them, as all could be excluded; but if these criteria are absent or flawed, one might establish relationships that later cause many avoidable problems.

After reflecting on the importance of knowing whom to court, one is ready to analyze the necessary qualities to detect and interpret the sexual signals a woman emits and determine one's feelings towards her.

~~~

Chapter 3: INTERPRETING A SEXUAL SIGNALS

In this chapter, we will analyze the sexual signals women give and the false positives that may arise when a woman seems open to romantic advances but is not truly interested. We will also explore the skills necessary to effectively detect and interpret these signals, as well as the importance of recognizing and understanding our own feelings during the process of courtship.

SIGNALS AND CLUES TO FOCUS YOUR ATTENTION

When the hen sings, it's because she wants the rooster. (Cuba)[102]

If a woman who is sexually attracted to you were to tell you directly that she's very interested in you and wants a romance, there wouldn't be much to interpret. But in our culture, such straightforwardness is rare. Typically, a woman expresses her intentions not so much through words but through nonverbal language, which, as previously explained, is predominantly unconscious. This means that often she herself isn't aware of the signals she's giving off, making her expressions sincere.

—Silence gives consent, a smile confirms it, and the body and eyes speak.

What are these signals? When a woman desires a romantic relationship but hasn't yet decided with whom, she often dresses more attractively, takes extra care in her appearance and makeup, tends to reference sexual topics in her conversation, and may become more uninhibited in her behavior.

—A neighing mare is calling for a stallion.

—The more she adorns herself, the more she wants something.

Once she becomes interested in someone in particular, she begins to send signals of sexual interest or attraction toward that person.

Next, we'll discuss both the signs of attraction and those that indicate disinterest, discomfort, or rejection. We'll also explore ways to recognize and interpret these signals.

HAIR AND HEAD SIGNALS

A- Signs of Interest or Sexual Attraction

- While looking at you, she plays with her hair or wraps it around her fingers.
- She repeatedly tosses her hair back over her shoulders.
- When listening to you, she slightly tilts her head to the side or nods it forward and backward.

B- Signs of Disinterest, Discomfort, or Rejection

- There are no noticeable changes in her behavior that indicate excitement or nervousness.
- She keeps her head upright and steady.

C- Exploration Methods

- Observe the woman's behavior when she notices your presence or when you're having a conversation with her.

EYE AND GAZE SIGNALS

A- Signs of Interest or Sexual Attraction

- From a distance, she frequently looks in your direction or gives you sidelong glances. The more frequent the glances, the better. This type of look is directed one way, while her body and face are turned another, indicating interest in something while trying not to be obvious. This often expresses sexual attraction, though it could also signify distrust or fear of something approaching.
- When your eyes meet, she lowers her gaze before looking away, as if embarrassed to be caught. Sometimes, she holds your gaze for a few seconds.
- If she's turned slightly away from you but maintains eye contact over her shoulder, smiles, and then looks away, she's challenging you to make a move.
- When close to you, her gaze moves across your entire face, not just your eyes, but also your lips, hair, cheekbones, etc. The more she looks at your mouth, the more likely she is attracted to you.
- She occasionally glances at parts of your body, such as your chest, shoulders, or buttocks.

- Her eyes appear brighter, and her pupils dilate. Generally, bright eyes indicate that she is very excited and happy in your presence.
- She stares deeply into your eyes, conveying strong interest in you, though it might not necessarily be sexual.
- She raises her eyebrows exaggeratedly for a couple of seconds and then lowers them, often accompanied by a smile and a look.
- She winks at you while talking or does so from a distance.
- When speaking to you, she blinks more frequently than usual, fluttering her eyelashes.

B- Signs of Disinterest, Discomfort, or Rejection

- She doesn't look at you.
- She avoids eye contact.
- When your eyes meet, she quickly looks away at eye level.

C- Exploration Methods

- Observe the woman's facial expression, particularly her eyes, when she looks at you, talks to you, or when your gazes meet.
- If she frequently watches you when your back is turned, you may need someone else to confirm it for you.

MOUTH SIGNALS

A- Signs of Interest or Sexual Attraction

- She bites or moistens her lips with her tongue.
- She adjusts her lips to make them appear fuller and more luscious. Some women may subconsciously associate their mouth with their genitalia, and by moistening their lips or making them look fuller, they might be unconsciously mimicking the appearance of their genitals when aroused.
- She runs her tongue over her front teeth. When she shows her tongue, especially the underside, it's often done with seductive intent.
- She smiles broadly, showing both her upper and lower teeth, while maintaining a relaxed expression.
- She plays with a fingernail by placing it between her teeth.

B- Signs of Disinterest, Discomfort, or Rejection

- She keeps a formal expression, and if she smiles, she does so with her lips tightly pressed together.

C- Exploration Methods

- Observe the woman's facial expression, particularly her mouth, when you talk or when she notices your presence.

NON-VERBAL SIGNALS WITH HER OWN VOICE

A- Signs of Interest or Sexual Attraction

- She raises or lowers the volume of her voice to match yours.
- She speeds up or slows down her speech to align with the way you speak.
- She begins to speak faster than usual, which might indicate that your presence is causing her some nervous excitement.

B- Signs of Disinterest, Discomfort, or Rejection

- There is no noticeable change in her usual manner of speaking.

C- Exploration Methods

- Observe any changes in the pitch, tone, and volume of her voice while she is talking to you.
- Sometimes, you may need to prompt her to speak or initiate a conversation to explore these signals further.

HAND SIGNALS

A- Signs of Interest or Sexual Attraction

- She shows you the palms of her hands.
- She adopts a position where one elbow rests on the palm of her hand while the other hand is extended with the palm facing up.
- She sits with one hand touching one of her breasts.
- She rubs her chin or touches her cheek.
- She caresses her keys, runs her hand up and down a glass, or generally uses objects on the table as toys.
- She plays with her earrings or bracelets, especially with forward and backward movements, which may unconsciously evoke sexual acts.
- She touches your arm, back, thigh, or hand while speaking to you.

B- Signs of Disinterest, Discomfort, or Rejection

- She clenches her fists.
- She bangs the table with her hands.

C- Exploration Methods

- Observe the gestures she makes with her hands while she notices your presence or while you're conversing with her.

SIGNALS WITH HER CLOTHING

A- Signs of Interest or Sexual Attraction:

- She adjusts her clothing to appear more attractive.
- She covers herself or changes position to avoid revealing body parts that her outfit might expose, such as her cleavage, stomach, navel, or thighs.

B- Signs of Disinterest, Discomfort, or Rejection:

- There are no noticeable changes in her behavior that would indicate excitement or nervousness.

C- Exploration Methods:

- Observe her behavior when she notices your presence.

SIGNALS WHILE SHE IS SITTING

A- Signs of Interest or Sexual Attraction:

- She moves to the rhythm of the music while locking eyes with you.
- She adopts an upright posture that accentuates her chest.
- She tenses her muscles to make them appear firm.
- She sits with her legs slightly apart or crossed in a way that exposes her thigh.
- She rubs her legs together or against the leg of the table.
- The leg she crosses over her knee points toward you, or she swings it back and forth in your direction.
- Both her pelvic waist and the line of her shoulders point toward you.
- While sitting, she positions herself so that you are within the angle created by her legs.
- When sitting across from you at a table, she removes objects between you two, so they don't serve as a barrier.

B- Signs of Disinterest, Discomfort, or Rejection:

- She sits so that both her pelvic waist and the line of her shoulders point in a direction away from you.
- She keeps her purse on her lap and holds onto it.
- She uses objects as barriers between you, for example: when sitting across from you at a table, she arranges bottles, vases, flowers, purses, etc., in a way that creates obstacles.

C- Exploration Methods:

- Observe her behavior when she is sitting in front of you.

- It may be necessary to ask her to sit or invite her to take a walk to elicit these signals. However, simply accepting an invitation to go out is already a very good sign.

OTHER SIGNALS

A- Signs of Interest or Sexual Attraction:

- She laughs at everything you say, even if it's not funny.
- She starts asking you all kinds of questions.
- She mirrors your body language and posture.
- She laughs at the same time as you.
- When she sees you, she changes to an alert posture, adjusts her clothes or hair, or shows any sign of nervousness.
- She blushes or seems nervous when she's near you.
- In a group, she talks only to you, focusing all her attention on you.
- She slightly tilts her head, with one foot behind the other and her hips slightly pointing towards you.
- She takes a stance where the tip of her shoe points towards you.
- At a party, she appears next to you from time to time, as if out of nowhere, and if you move to another spot, she soon shows up there too.
- If you're talking and go to greet some friends or go to the bathroom, she stays in the same place when you return.
- If she needs to greet friends or go to the bathroom, she comes right back to your side afterward.
- If you reach for something and get close enough to touch her, she doesn't move away. The more active version of this is when she expresses her interest by "accidentally" touching you with her body. These signs indicate that she feels physically comfortable around you.
- She takes a posture that emphasizes her chest.
- If you dance a slow song together, she ends up leaning on you.
- She avoids directly showing her interest, but doesn't stray too far from you.
- She reacts aggressively or treats you with unusual roughness that seems like mistreatment. Aggressive behavior may stem from feeling emotionally vulnerable and trying to hide this fragility through a tough exterior. However, it could also be a sincere expression of strong rejection.

B- Signs of Disinterest, Discomfort, or Rejection:

- She hunches her shoulders inward to deemphasize her chest.
- She turns her body away from you, aligning her legs and hips in a different direction.
- When she sees you, she doesn't adjust her clothes or hair, nor does she show any sign of nervousness.
- When you start talking, her posture doesn't change.
- Her head and torso remain upright and rigid.
- If you get too close or touch her, she pulls back defensively.
- You leave to greet friends or go to the bathroom, and when you return, she's no longer there. (Did she vanish?)
- She greets some friends and doesn't return to your side.
- She refuses to dance with you, or if she does and it's a slow song, she uses her forearms as a barrier to keep you from getting too close.

C- Exploration Methods:

- Observe the woman's behavior when you touch her, dance with her, or invite her to dance.

These are some signals or indications of a woman's sexual attitude; through which she expresses with her body what is going on in her mind.

By the thread, you find the ball of yarn. (Spain)[103]

−By the trail, you find the hare. (Spain)[104]

−The smoke shows where the fire is.

−By the suitcase, you identify the passenger. (Cuba)[105]

It's important to clarify that a single signal can have multiple interpretations, and not all signals are expressed in the same way or with the same intensity. Additionally, it's worth noting that a woman's sexual attitude toward someone is not static; it can change depending on the direction the relationship takes.

False Positives

There are instances where a woman may exhibit clear signs of sexual attraction, but when approached, even with the right technique, her attitude shifts to outright rejection. This can happen because, although the man may be sexually appealing to her, pursuing a romantic relationship with him might present significant social complications that she is unwilling to face.

In other cases, a woman may behave seductively without feeling genuine sexual attraction, possibly because she needs a service that the man can provide and believes that acting seductively will help her obtain it more quickly or with better results. Additionally, she might have a pathologically strong need for affirmation and to be the center of attention, or she might derive a perverse pleasure from arousing a man's desire only to reject him afterward.

–Appearances can be deceiving.

–Don't judge a tree by its bark.

If you attempt to pursue a romantic relationship with women who exhibit these characteristics, particularly the latter two, it's likely that you'll experience significant discomfort. Therefore, it's crucial to recognize these behaviors early on so you can either halt your efforts or know what to expect.

Weak Points

Weak Points Are Keys to a Woman's Heart

Every human being has weak points that act as gateways to their will. The ability to detect and utilize these is a valuable social skill in courtship, allowing for significant time savings.

–You don't breach a castle through its strongest wall.

45

−Everyone has their Achilles' heel.

But what exactly are these weak points, and how can you discover them? Generally, they are the main motives and needs that govern a woman's life— what she loves, likes, or what gives her security, as well as what she dislikes, hates, or makes her feel insecure.

−It's important to know how to approach a woman and with what.

−Every beast has its side to be mounted.

−You must find the grain in the wood, the vein in the stone, and the way to approach a woman. (Mexico)[106]

You can learn about a woman's weak points first by observing her and detecting the signals she emits with her entire body; second, by conversing with her or subtly drawing out information; and third, by investigating, although this should be done cautiously to avoid revealing your intentions to potential competition.

Once a woman's weak points are known, the next step is to work on them and focus on these areas with words and temptations.

−Give where there is need. (China)[107]

However, just as it is important to detect a woman's weak points, it is equally crucial to know your own best qualities or resources and use them wisely. If these align with her weak points, the chances of success could be high.

QUALITIES NECESSARY TO DETECT A WOMAN'S SEXUAL SIGNALS

Detecting and correctly interpreting a woman's sexual signals, which include subtle gestures, words, and behaviors, requires several essential qualities and skills. Among these, empathy stands out as it allows you to see things from another person's perspective; discernment and objectivity, which help in evaluating the signals clearly and without bias; and last but not least, the ability for introspection, which aids in understanding your own emotions and reactions.

Ability to See Things from Others' Perspectives

One thing thinks the donkey, and another thinks the one who is saddling it. (Colombia)[108]

If there's one quality that's crucial for achieving success in life in general and in courting in particular, it's the ability to see things from others' perspectives and infer what they think and feel, putting yourself in their shoes as if you were in the same situation.[109]

–*Without empathy, no matter how many other qualities you have, you won't go far.*

–*Before you do something, think about how you would feel if it were done to you.*

Not everyone thinks and feels the same about the same things, for various reasons, including that their interests and relationships with those things differ.

–*So many heads, so many reasons. (Czech Republic)[110]*

–*One thing thinks the drunk, and another thinks the bartender.*

−Foolish is the one who thinks others don't think. (Spain)[111]

But when people have similar relationships with things, their interests and ways of thinking and feeling about them tend to have similarities. Because of this, if we take as reference points the interests we would have and how we would think and feel if we were in the same situation as the woman, we can get a good approximation of her inner world. Then, what has been inferred should be corroborated through other methods such as observation, inquiry, and probing, which were briefly discussed in the previous topic.

One weakness of this approach is that if our inner world has distortions, we will tend to infer that these are also present in others, even when this is not always the case.

− The wicked always think they are being deceived.

− The thief thinks that everyone steals. (Danish Saying)[112]

− The thief believes everyone else is of the same nature. (Spain)[113]

Discernimiento y objetividad

Call bread, bread, and wine, wine. (Spain)[114]

Two elements of great importance when it comes to detecting and interpreting a woman's sexual signals are discernment and objectivity. The first consists of knowing how to distinguish something from other things, pointing out the differences between them. The second lies in sticking to reality and the facts, which allows you to see things as they truly are—a requirement for discernment.

− Things by their name.

Catathymia and Self-Deception as Vices of Objectivity

There is a wide variety of ways in which objectivity is lost, through which an individual, in a largely unconscious manner, alters how they perceive reality to accommodate their self-esteem, transforming or inhibiting that perception.[115] In this work, only catathymia and self-deception will be discussed. In the former, the alteration of perception occurs due to emotions, causing things to be perceived not as they truly are, but as we wish or fear them to be.

When it comes to love, especially if passion is strong, it is often difficult to be objective and make impartial judgments.

–*The more one loves, the less one judges.*

–*Love, like fear, makes everything believable.*

–*To love and to know, both together cannot be. (Spain)[116]*

–*Love, hate, and fear all exaggerate.*

To one who loves an ugly person, they seem beautiful.

The above is important because passionate love brings out the best in each person, and it helps us overlook small flaws in the other person. And if there is reciprocity, they too will overlook our small flaws.

–*For the lover's eyes, smallpox scars are charming dimples. (Japan)[117]*

–*The lover, in what they love, finds no imperfections. (Mexico)[118]*

The problem begins when the alteration in the ability to perceive reality is so intense that it prevents one from seeing significant flaws in the other person, which can cause great harm.

–*When passions blind, reasoning is unnecessary. (Spain)[119]*

−Full of passion, empty of reason. (Mexico)[120]

−A passionate heart does not want to be advised.

−Affection blinds reason. (Spain)[121]

−Where the heart is king, its command cannot be disobeyed. (Afro-Cuban Saying)[122]

−Only a fool will see affection in a harsh girl, sweetness in one who is cruel, and feeling in one who has no heart. (Panchatantra)[123]

The lack of objectivity due to emotions can cause someone to overvalue supposed signs of attraction and underestimate or deny signs of rejection, leading to the invention of unfounded hopes or assuming something is certain when it still needs time to mature or has no possibilities at the moment.

−We haven't saddled up yet, and we're already riding. (Spain)[124]

−Stories don't fill the belly. (Galicia, Spain)[125]

−The belly doesn't get full with hope. (Colombia)[126]

−You can't fill your belly by painting bread. (China)[127]

−Fantasy after fantasy, and the belly stays empty. (Spain)[128]

There is no worse blind person than the one who does not want to see.

In self-deception, the interpretation of reality and memories are altered to avoid elements that are painful,[129] which creates a disconnect from the facts.

−You can't cover the sun with a finger.

−Some people act like an ostrich, burying their head in the sand to avoid seeing things.

−Ignoring reality doesn't make it go away.

Failing to recognize and address real problems can lead to failure in achieving goals.

Better a bird in the hand than a hundred in the bush. (Spain)[130]

It's important to clarify that it doesn't mean you have to constantly stay "connected" to a painful reality, which would be a form of self-punishment, or stop having dreams, which would make life very dull. However, to deliberate and make appropriate decisions, you need to be as objective as possible.

–*Wars are only won with feet on the ground. (Afro-Cuban Saying)[131]*

–*Head on your shoulders and feet on the ground. (Afro-Cuban Saying)[132]*

–*Better a sparrow in the hand than a hundred geese flying. (England)[133]*

CAPACITY FOR INTROSPECTION

Being able to interpret a woman's sexual signals is a useful skill, but it's not enough to ensure a successful courtship. Relying solely on this ability can lead us to form dysfunctional relationships that, in the long run, could cause us significant pain. It's crucial to be aware of our own feelings toward the woman. Often, the deciding factor in not starting or stopping a romantic pursuit is simply not feeling good when interacting with that person.

– Where you don't feel comfortable, don't linger.

– It's better to be alone than in bad company.

No matter how much we are attracted to a woman, or how many good qualities we see in her, if during the initial phase of courtship, when the bonds are still weak, we already experience discomfort, it is most likely that this will intensify as the relationship deepens. In this context, if the courtship process, which should be enjoyable, actually causes discomfort, it's worth asking: does it make sense to continue pursuing this relationship?

– Withdrawing in time is a victory.

FINAL CONSIDERATIONS

This chapter could be defined as semiological, focusing on the ability to interpret a woman's sexual signals and your own evolving feelings as the courtship progresses. It can be said that:

–Any action aimed at winning a woman's love, if carried out without considering her sexual signals and weak spots, would be like operating blindly.

–A highly valuable social skill, both in life generally and especially during courtship, is the ability to put yourself in someone else's shoes and infer what they might be thinking and feeling, imagining how you would feel and think if you were in the same situation.

–It's wise to know and cultivate your best qualities or resources for courting and use them intelligently. If these align with the woman's weak spots, the chances of success can be high.

–It's important to look inward and understand what you think and feel towards the woman, whether it's sexual attraction or any other type. Sometimes, the only necessary reason to decide not to start or to stop courting someone is simply that you don't feel right with her.

However, knowing how to detect and interpret a woman's sexual signals isn't enough to make courtship effective, since it is, at its core, an interpersonal relationship. Therefore, it's essential to know how to interact appropriately with others.

~~~

53

Chapter 4: INTERACTING WITH OTHERS

In this fourth chapter, we will discuss the qualities necessary for interacting appropriately with other people.

CIVILITY

If there is one activity where it's crucial to have skills for interacting properly with others, it's courtship. The absence of these skills can even be a dealbreaker for many women. Moreover, if the woman exhibits inappropriate behaviors in this regard, it should serve as a signal for the suitor to reflect on whether to continue or stop his efforts to win her over.

Among these qualities is civility, which encompasses them all, along with its components: courtesy, tact, flattery, generosity, discretion, decorum, self-confidence, and a sense of humor, among many others.

Civility is the set of social skills and refinements that allow for proper interaction with others. It includes not only good manners and treatment of others but also the care of communication in all its aspects: language, hygiene, demeanor, and personal appearance, among others—elements that were discussed in the section "Communication and Courtship."

Although these qualities are not exclusively erotic, they are culturally accepted ways through which one can effectively attract a sexual partner.

At one vicious extreme of civility lies the rudeness and indelicacy of those who lack basic social refinements; at the other extreme is the excess of consideration in social behavior, as well as the passivity and weakness of those who allow others to take advantage of them.

It is important to note that what works as effective courtship in one culture or subculture may be offensive and counterproductive in others, so it is advisable to keep these differences in mind and adapt accordingly.

COURTESY

You reap what you sow. (Spain)[134]

This quality consists of the demonstration or act of showing attention, respect, or affection towards others, which creates the foundation for being treated the same way by them.

—*As you sow, so shall you reap.*

—*Every action has a reaction.*

It helps achieve very valuable goals, and applying it costs nothing.

—*Courtesy costs nothing and achieves much.*

—*Speaking kindly doesn't harm the tongue. (France)[135]*

During courtship, this quality paves the way to winning the favor of women, who generally appreciate men who know how to treat others well. This is because it is assumed that they will be able to handle the various situations that may arise in a potential family, and more importantly, they will be capable of treating them well.

—*Courtesy and good speech will open a hundred doors. (Spain)[136]*

—*Good appearance and good manners open main doors. (Spain)[137]*

Discourtesy and Rudeness

If you want to gather honey, don't kick the beehive.[138]

At the vicious extreme by default lie discourtesy and rudeness, where one does not observe civility in their words or actions and behaves disrespectfully, thus earning the ill will of others. During courtship, these are highly despised qualities by women and are often reasons for exclusion.

– *You can't ripen fruits by hitting them.*

– *Discourtesy is a closed door.*

– *A little bitterness can spoil a lot of sweetness. (Spain)[139]*

– *Discourtesy is the poison of coexistence.*

– *If you sow thorns, don't expect to harvest flowers.*

Passivity and Weakness

The gentle donkey is loaded with more weight.

At the other vicious extreme lie the passivity and weakness of those who struggle to set boundaries in their relationships and allow others to take advantage of them.

– The one that is made honey is eaten with fingers.(Panama)[140]

– He who makes himself honey is eaten by ants. (Cuba)[141]

– He who makes himself a lamb is eaten by the wolf. (Italy)[142]

– He who plays dumb gets skewered. (Cuba)[143]

– Excessive kindness is called foolishness. (San Salvador)[144]

– There will always be someone who abuses the unfortunate.

– Everyone climbs the low wall. (Arab Saying)[145]

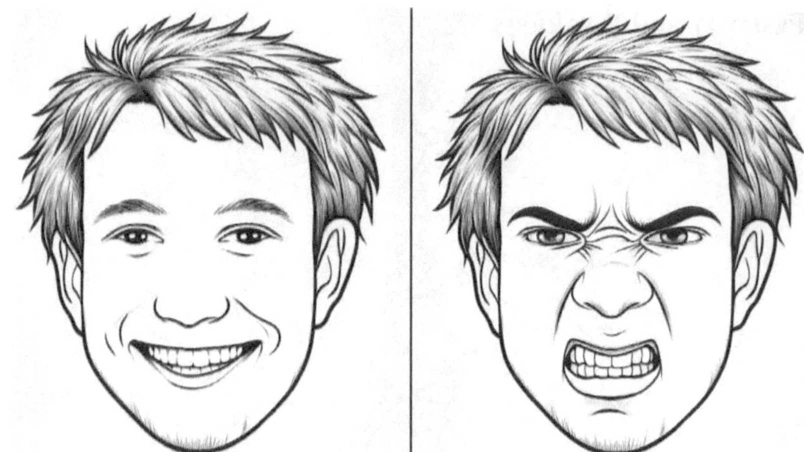

There is a time to be affable and a time to be irascible.

For behavior to be effective, it must be adjusted to the demands of the circumstances. It's not about always being polite, affable, or kind; it's important to know when to become irascible when necessary.

- *There is a time to embrace and a time to refrain from embracing. (Ecclesiastes 3:5)[146]*

It's good for a woman to know that, no matter how devoted you are to her, there are limits to the treatment you are willing to tolerate and the lengths you are willing to go to win or maintain her love.

- *Being courteous doesn't mean allowing yourself to be trampled on.*

- *It's your responsibility to set healthy boundaries.*

- *Healthy boundaries are necessary.*

TACT

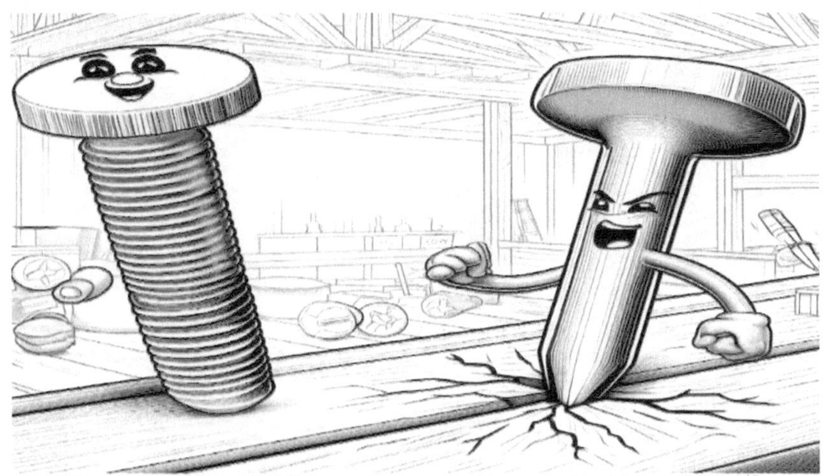

You should go in like a screw, not like a nail. (Colombia)[147]

This quality refers to the prudence or caution needed to approach a delicate matter, such as romantic courtship.

−Those who tread softly go far. (China)[148]

−He who doesn't tire, reaches his goal. (Spain)[149]

−With tact and care, you achieve what you desire.

Tact is demonstrated in various ways during courtship, two very important ones being: applying the so-called "iron theory" and respecting personal boundaries.

Iron Theory

Will I Get Burned if I Touch It?

If someone is standing in front of an iron and doesn't know its temperature or whether they might get burned by touching it, how could they find out? First, they might quickly tap it, which will give them an initial impression to guide them, but that won't be enough. Next, they might touch it for a slightly longer time and then pull their hand back to see if they got burned. This way, they touch it for increasingly longer periods until they realize there's no danger of getting burned, and then they can safely grab it.

If, instead of an iron, the person is in front of a woman and doesn't know her level of openness towards him, he can approach and withdraw, observing her responses at each moment. If the responses are positive, he can gradually increase the intensity, both in conversation and physical contact. However, if the responses are negative, they indicate where the boundary lies, and he should avoid making further advances for the time being.

Safety Distance

We All Have a Perimeter Around Us That We Consider Our
Personal Space

All human beings have a perimeter around them that they perceive as their personal space or safety distance, and they feel uncomfortable if someone who is not emotionally close enters it.[150] Although this space varies from person to person, it generally comprises the distance of an outstretched arm and tends to be shorter in people living in urban areas compared to those in rural areas.

If someone has a very short safety distance and approaches a woman who doesn't know him yet, it may make her feel uncomfortable and generate rejection if his personal space is much smaller than hers.

Indelicacy

Some people are as delicate as an elephant in a china shop.

One of the vicious extremes of tact is the indelicacy of someone who acts without any consideration in matters that, due to their fragility, require it, and ends up causing rejection.

 −*He who is indelicate will be avoided.*

 −*The indelicate person reaps displeasure.*

 −*Rudeness is the mother of isolation.*

Shyness

The hawk doesn't ask the dove for permission to hunt it.

At the other extreme is the person who has so many unnecessary hesitations and inhibitions that they end up taking no action and leave important needs unmet.

- *Do not show consideration to others to your own detriment, and do not be ashamed to save yourself from ruin. (Ecclesiasticus 4:22)[151]*
- *It's useless to ask the cow, "Please do me a favor and give me a glass of milk." (United States)[152]*
- *Oysters don't open by persuasion.*

Sometimes, the methods required by circumstances are very different from those one is accustomed to, and having irrational ideas or unproductive reservations about them makes it difficult to carry them out. However, they must be executed if one wants to succeed.

- *A merciful surgeon never made a good cure.*
- *You can't make an omelet without breaking eggs.*

REFINED PRAISE

Tell her she's beautiful and you'll pop a candy in her mouth.

Refined praise is the ability to offer compliments that genuinely satisfy and subtly elevate egos, delivered with sweetness and grace. Those skilled in this art know how to make others feel valued without resorting to insincere flattery or excessive sweetness.

–*Sweet talk is the art of success. (Spain)*[153]

–*A good word is a golden key. (Bulgaria)*[154]

–*A sweet tongue is worth a lot. (Romania)*[155]

–*Some things are bought with kind words, not money.*

True merit is celebrated, and even if a well-timed compliment doesn't lead to romance, it's always welcomed.

–*The pleasure of praise reaches everyone.*

–*Tell a woman she's pretty, and the devil will repeat it ten times.*

–*Tell her she's beautiful, and you can ask her for anything. (Mexico)*[156]

Sometimes, a woman might not spontaneously show signs of acceptance or rejection, and one way to gauge her disposition is by celebrating her qualities and observing her reaction to compliments. In this context, flattery serves a diagnostic purpose. If the signals are positive, you can gradually increase the intensity of the compliments and other expressions of interest until it reaches the physical level. In this regard, flattery has a therapeutic function.

–*The flattering tongue can make one slip.*[157]

A playful way to celebrate feminine beauty is through compliments, which are discussed at the end of this book.

Compliments and Exclusivity

A high level of complimenting a woman's qualities is achieved when you make her feel unique to you. She feels not only loved, desired, missed, and sought after, but also the one who has captivated you the most, made you feel the best, or understood you the deepest. In short, making her feel very special and extraordinarily important.

−Love thrives on exclusivity.

−Love does not tolerate competition.

This principle works similarly for men, who also enjoy feeling special and exclusive in their relationship with a woman.

Coldness

A dry finger can't lift salt. (China)[158]

In the vicious extreme of refined praise by defect lies the coldness of someone who struggles to express admiration or affection for a woman, making courtship very difficult.

−A cold heart doesn't ignite passion.

−Cold love doesn't warm the soul.

−Ice in the heart kills passion.

Flattery, Cloying Sweetness, and Vulgarity

In the vicious extremes of excess are flattery, cloying sweetness, and vulgarity. Flattery involves saying what might please a woman but excessively or praising qualities she knows she doesn't have, which sounds false and creates rejection or distrust.

−Excessive praise sounds like a lie.

−Too many compliments raise suspicion.

−False flattery breeds distrust.

Cloying is about causing irritation or discomfort through untimely expressions of affection or persistently insisting despite a woman's clear rejection, sometimes even when she responds harshly.

−Too much sweetness cloys. (Afro-Cuban Saying)[159]

−Even nectar is poison if taken in excess. (India)[160]

−Don't squeeze the orange so much that the juice turns bitter. (Colombia)[161]

−Women and oranges, if squeezed too much, turn bitter. (Spain)[162]

Vulgarity lies in crude and tasteless words or actions, which instead of winning a woman's favor, provoke rejection.

GENEROSITY

A gift is something given or a service offered graciously, representing an investment without a guaranteed return, but it often wins the favor of the recipient.

- *Gifts can break stones. (Spain)*[163]
- *Gifts and kind words soften stones and hearts. (Spain)*[164]
- *Give a wing, and you'll eat the breast. (San Salvador)*[165]
- *By giving and speaking well, you win hearts. (Quevedo)*[166]
- *Whoever satisfies others will be satisfied.*[167]

Generosity is the quality of someone inclined to give gifts and knows how to do so gracefully.

- *The way of giving is worth more than what is given.*

Stinginess

As a vicious extreme by defect, there is the one who ridiculously skimps on expenses to attend to a woman, which is stinginess.

- *A miser's gift seems like it belongs to him. (Spain)*[168]
- *Hands that don't give, what do you seek? (Galicia, Spain)*[169]
- *A saint who doesn't perform miracles remains in the dark. (Spain)*[170]
- *Great prosperity doesn't come if small generosity doesn't go. (China)*[171]

Cloying

Give unexpected little details, but don't overwhelm her with gifts.

Both through refined praise and generosity, a suitor demonstrates his affection and interest in a woman. However, an excess of either can lead to cloying.

−Praise and gifts have their dosage and timing.

The goal of a gift, especially in the early stages of a relationship, is not to meet the woman's material needs, but to show interest in her and in courting her. Simple gifts are enough; sometimes, a single flower can achieve this purpose.

−Nothing in excess.

If the gift is untimely, excessively expensive, or extravagant, it can give the impression of desperation to win her over. Instead of making her feel special, it overwhelms her and creates distrust. Rather than attracting her, it may cause her to distance herself. Additionally, the woman might keep an emotional distance, expecting that the gifts will stop once the conquest is achieved, and thus continue receiving them.

−Excesses lead to nothing good.

Everything in its time. (Spain)[172]

Expressions of attention and affection—whether through compliments, gifts, or services—should be dosed appropriately. While sometimes they should be offered promptly, at other times, they should be withheld.

–*Everything in its moment.*

–*Everything in its time. (Spain)[173]*

–*The wise... in their actions, love finding the right moment. (Lao Tzu)[174]*

–*In this world, everything has its hour; there is a time for everything that happens. (Ecclesiastes 3:1)[175]*

DISCRETION

Learn to keep quiet well, so you may know how to speak well.
(Spain)[176]

One highly valued quality, especially by women, is discretion, which can be defined as the art of acting, speaking, or remaining silent with wit and timeliness. This topic emphasizes the importance of knowing when to stay silent.

–*He who knows nothing else knows enough if he knows when to keep silent. (Italy)[177]*

–*Some things are better done than said. (Spain)[178]*

Women often protect their reputation and avoid illicit relationships due to potential social consequences. Therefore, when they learn that a man has the habit of bragging about his conquests and boasting of his "feats," they will know that being involved with him leads to undesirable outcomes, making this a strong reason to dismiss him.

–*A woman-hunting hawk has no bells.*

–*A talkative suitor is a poor suitor and an even worse gentleman.*

Discretion in courtship is crucial not only in keeping quiet about what has been done but also about what is planned. If you reveal your intentions to potential competitors, you might inadvertently spark their interest in the woman, leading them to act before you do.

–*The hen loses her nest by clucking. (Cuba)[179]*

–*Guard your words, and you guard yourself; the talkative will ruin themselves. (Proverbs 13:3)[180]*

–*He who talks much, advances little. (Romania)[181]*

–The one who talks much puts himself in danger. (Afro-Cuban Saying)[182]

–He who reveals what he has may lose it. (Afro-Cuban Saying)[183]

The lack of discretion in others can be used to your advantage. If someone shows interest in a woman you are also interested in, you can diminish their enthusiasm by criticizing their choice and making negative remarks about the lady's beauty. Likewise, be cautious when seeking advice in matters of love, as your interests may conflict with those of the advisor, who may give suggestions that benefit themselves and harm you.

–Do not consult with your rivals, and hide your plans from those who envy you. (Sirach 37:10)[184]

–Be wary of advisors; consider what they need, for they may also counsel for their own benefit. (Sirach 37:8)[185]

Indiscretion

The fish dies by its mouth. (Spain)[186]

This quality refers to the lack of tact or timing when acting or speaking, revealing information that should be kept secret.

–The fool neither knows when to speak nor when to stay silent. (Czechoslovakia)[187]

–The milkman wasn't killed for watering down the milk but for talking about it.

–He who talks too much condemns himself. (Afro-Cuban Saying)[188]

–Better a misstep with the feet than with the tongue. (Sirach 20:18)[189]

Don't talk about the good things. (Afro-Cuban Saying)[190]

When a man boasts about his "countless conquests" to others, he often recounts the same relationship in different ways, giving the impression of numerous affairs. This behavior not only risks him being rejected by women but also stirs the pride of his listeners, often leading to envy and its negative consequences.

–*Not staying silent about one's happiness gives birth to envy.*

–*No one should say they are loved, even if they are adored.*

Retreat and Timidity

On the opposite end of discretion lie retreat and timidity. Retreat refers to shrinking back and being less communicative in situations where communication is necessary.

–*A silent mouth, God does not hear. (Spain)[191]*

–*A baby that doesn't cry, doesn't nurse. (Spain)[192]*

–*It's bad to stay silent when it's time to speak.*

–*Do not refrain from speaking when necessary. (Sirach 4:23)[193]*

–*Wisdom is knowing when to keep silent until it's time to speak. (Spain)[194]*

It's not about always staying silent, but about knowing when to speak and when to hold back.

–*Let us be like bells that ring when it's time and remain silent when it's time. (Spain)[195]*

Timidity in relation to discretion involves an excessive hesitation to speak or act, leading to missed necessary actions or lost opportunities due to overthinking.

– *If you have the chance and don't take it due to lack of courage, don't complain when it's gone. (Quevedo)*[196]

– *When opportunity knocks, open the door.*

– *Once the opportunity is gone, it's in vain to chase it. (Egypt)*[197]

ROMANTICISM

A romantic suitor evokes tender or loving feelings in the lady by either seeking or creating favorable circumstances that inspire these emotions, expressing his love and admiration in an elegant, deep, and distinguished manner, or through "little acts of madness" that make the woman feel special and unique.

Coldness

As with lisonja, one of the vices of romanticism is difficulty expressing admiration or love for the woman, which is highly detrimental in courtship.

Sentimentality and Corniness

On the other hand, there is the one who is overly exaggerated or hasty in expressing affection, which is sentimentality. Similarly, someone who attempts to be elegant, deep, distinguished, or refined but fails, coming across as ridiculous or in bad taste, is being corny.

Courtship is a journey that both must walk step by step, progressively increasing the level of actions while carefully observing the other's responses. When one notices that the other is pausing, it's time to consider doing the same and wait for them to move forward again. If they don't, it may be time to let go of pursuing a love that isn't reciprocated.

—For unrequited love, absence and forgetfulness. (Spain)[198]

—For disdain, forgetfulness. (Mexico)[199]

—Learn to offer your absence to those who don't value your presence.

—It's pointless to fight when love isn't mutual. (Mexico)[200]

Moving too quickly or showing affection too intensely for the current stage of the relationship doesn't make a woman feel special. Instead, it may make her feel undeserving of such affection and fearful that the relationship might become overly controlling. This is a key reason why she might choose not to continue advancing in the relationship.

—Be romantic, but not foolishly romantic.

DECORUM

An essential quality for building relationships, and thus progressing in courtship, is decorum. This involves self-respect, closely tied to healthy self-esteem and self-love. The way others treat us is greatly influenced by how we view and treat ourselves, so to be loved and respected by others, we must first love and respect ourselves.

–Value yourself so that others will value you. (Cuba)[201]

If someone is rejected to the point of mistreatment yet continues to pursue or maintain that relationship, they end up generating contempt.

–Respect fosters love; one who is scorned cannot be loved. (José Martí)[202]

–The one who begs for love without self-respect will receive neither love nor respect.

–If you tolerate everything, don't be surprised if you're treated like a doormat.

Indecorum

Do not enslave yourself to a woman to the point where she
tramples on you. (Sirach 9:2)[203]

One of the vicious extremes of decorum is indecorum, which involves a lack of self-respect often tied to low self-esteem and feelings of inferiority.

The indecorous person will do anything to obtain or maintain a woman's love.

–He who bows too much shows his rear. (Sephardic Jewish Saying)[204]

–One who does not respect themselves invites misfortune. (China)[205]

Arrogance

On the other vicious extreme lies arrogance, an exaggerated sense of self-love born from the belief in one's personal superiority, often accompanied by a disdain for the qualities and merits of others.

–*He who falls in love with himself will have no rivals. (Benjamin Franklin)*[206]

–*Everything can be feigned except self-esteem. (José Martí)*[207]

–*The wise man loves himself but does not exalt himself. (Lao Tzu)*[208]

The arrogant person isolates themselves for several reasons; one of them is their disdainful and inconsiderate treatment of others, which can be hurtful.

–*Pride leads to loneliness.*

–*Humility attracts goodwill, while arrogance drives it away.*

–*As long as you sow pride, you will continue to reap isolation.*

Though they point in different directions, both arrogance and lack of self-respect greatly affect interpersonal relationships, including courtship. While a lack of self-love can generate contempt, an excess makes a person hard to tolerate.

SELF-CONFIDENCE

Self-confidence allows us to fully utilize the resources we truly possess.

It is the feeling of adequacy and the belief that we can successfully face various life situations and demands. This feeling arises from the conviction that we have the necessary resources and abilities to do so.[209]

This quality doesn't expand our potential but enables us to maximize what we already have. Someone who leaps over a tall fence with agility when chased by a dog isn't doing something beyond their abilities—they're just using their capacities without inhibition.

—Without self-confidence, we are only a part of ourselves.

Behaviors that demonstrate self-confidence inspire others' trust in us and are highly attractive to women.[210]

—Trust yourself, and others will trust you too.

Insecurity

On the vicious extreme of deficiency lies the feeling of inadequacy when facing certain situations and demands of life. When self-confidence is lacking, we don't fully utilize our resources and abilities because we are too focused on battling internal obstacles. Often, our potential is more than enough to achieve our goals.

—Fear, doubt, and self-distrust weaken a person's faculties.

A person who lacks self-confidence shows insecurity in their words and body language, which prevents others from trusting them and invites rejection.

—He who asks without faith invites refusal.

–If you don't trust yourself, who will?

–He who lacks sufficient faith will not be entrusted with the faith of others. (Lao Tzu)[211]

False Self-Confidence

If someone believes they are something when they are nothing,
they deceive themselves. (Galatians 6:3)[212]

On the vicious extreme of excess lies false self-confidence, where one believes they possess resources and abilities they don't actually have. This often leads to setting goals that are far beyond their real capabilities.

–He who does not know his limitations overreaches and fails. (Afro-Cuban Saying)[213]

Perceptions of what one can achieve aren't always accurate, and this error is usually corrected through practice and experience. Sometimes, we're surprised by what we can actually do.

–One learns what they are capable of by trying.

However, if one struggles to correct these errors in judgment, they will face many disappointments when confronted with reality.

–He who refuses to listen to reason will surely feel its blows.

–He who insists on making an impossible dream come true will fail. (Afro-Cuban Saying)[214]

SENSE OF HUMOR

Don't open a shop unless you like to smile. (China)[215]

This quality is the ability to see, judge, or comment on reality by highlighting the funny, cheerful, or ridiculous aspects of things. During courtship, it has several benefits, such as conveying an optimistic view of life, enhancing communication and emotional connection,[216] and reducing the tensions that typically arise during romantic pursuits.[217]

It also makes the company of someone with a good sense of humor fun and enjoyable, indicating good mental and physical health as well as intelligence—qualities highly valued by the opposite sex. For all these reasons, a good sense of humor can be considered almost aphrodisiacal.

A refined social skill, it usually comes with timing, authenticity, and sensitivity. Without these, it can devolve into various negative forms, including:

On the extreme of deficiency or absence, there is a lack of humor in those who are overly serious, making it difficult for them to see the comedic side of reality, which makes their company dull.

– Without laughter, life is gray.

The desire to appear funny sometimes prevents one from actually being funny.

On the excessive side of humor, there are several distortions, including:

The inopportune joker who tries to be funny in situations where jokes are unwelcome.

−Where everyone leaves crying, I can't go in singing. (Spain)[218]

−Neither laugh where they cry, nor cry where they laugh. (Spain)[219]

−Everything in its time, and humor in its moment.

The one who makes jokes so disconnected from the woman's experience that they are incomprehensible and not amusing to her.

−Study the humor of people and adapt to each.

Inauthentic humor that sounds forced or desperate to please.

−Fake laughter doesn't reach the soul.

−Empty laughter doesn't fill the heart.

−False laughter is a shadow without the sun.

Vulgar or coarse humor that feels like offensive mockery.

−Vulgar humor, rather than being funny, brings sorrow.

−A vulgar joke, rather than entertaining, offends.

With vulgarity and coarseness, one ultimately reveals a lack of refinement and culture.

−A coarse joke reveals a lack of culture.

−Those who laugh with vulgarity tarnish their reputation in society.

−Where there is crudeness, elegance is lost.

−Coarseness does not adorn; rather, it diminishes.

FINAL CONSIDERATIONS

Since courtship is essentially an interpersonal relationship, the qualities necessary for effective interaction with others, such as politeness and its components, are indispensable. In this regard, it can be said that:

−Politeness is the set of social skills and refinements that allow individuals to interact appropriately with others. It includes not only good manners and treatment of others but also the care of both verbal and non-verbal communication in all its aspects.

−At one extreme of politeness is the rudeness and lack of social refinement of those who lack basic social skills; at the other is an excess of caution in social behavior, leading to passivity and weakness, allowing others to take advantage.

−Some components of politeness include:

- o **Courtesy**: A gesture or act that shows attention, respect, or affection towards another person.
- o **Tact**: Prudence or caution in handling delicate matters.
- o **Flattery**: The quality of being prone to praise to win someone's favor.
- o **Generosity**: The ability to give gifts or services gracefully.
- o **Discretion**: The art of acting, speaking, or remaining silent with cleverness and timeliness.
- o **Dignity**: A sense of self-respect.
- o **Self-confidence**: The feeling of adequacy and the belief that one can successfully face certain situations and life's demands.
- o **Sense of humor**: The ability to see, judge, or comment on reality by highlighting the humorous, amusing, or ridiculous side of things.

−Politeness and its components are vital in any type of interpersonal relationship, even more so in courtship, where both sexes mutually evaluate these social skills. A lack of these in one participant may lead to exclusion by the other.

Relating well with others is crucial for effective courtship, but it is not enough. It's also necessary to know how to exercise self-control when circumstances require it.

~~~

Chapter 5. ADEQUATE SELF-CONTROL

In this chapter, we will discuss self-control and its components: boldness, perseverance, patience, readiness, equanimity, and resignation. Additionally, we will explore the specific application of each within the context of courtship.

SELF-CONTROL

This quality is the ability to overcome inclinations or aversions in situations where it is necessary to do so.

–Only he who commands himself, commands others. (José Martí)[220]

–Great is the king who rules himself well. (Desiderius Erasmus)[221]

–Better to conquer oneself than to conquer cities. (Proverbs 16:32)[222]

One form of self-control is continence, which is the ability to refrain from doing something you greatly desire but know will have negative consequences or ruin your plans. This quality includes the ability to delay gratification when circumstances are not ideal.

–Let's learn to say "No" to ourselves.

Another important form of self-control is the ability to self-motivate when circumstances require it, and to perform necessary tasks, even if they are undesirable or unpleasant.

–Say "Yes" when you need to say "Yes," and "No" when you need to say "No."

–Yes for yes and no for no is all the wisdom I know.

–Appetites must obey reason; they should neither outrun it nor abandon it due to weakness or laziness. (Marcus Tullius Cicero)[223]

–Don't wait for the light to go out to look for matches. (Cuba)[224]

–Dig the well before you're thirsty. (China)[225]

–When the antelope is in front of you, it's not the time to make the spear. (Guinea)[226]

–When you're thirsty, it's too late to dig a well. (Japan)[227]

–The strong foresee; second-rate men await the storm with folded arms. (José Martí)[228]

There is self-control in the face of anger, fear, fatigue, hunger, sleep, and even love; all its forms are crucial during courtship. This is because, during the phase of romantic pursuit, there is a mutual evaluation of each other's qualities, and vices related to self-control are significant causes of rejection.

Why is self-control over love important if we constantly hear that this feeling is extraordinarily good? What need could there be to exercise control over ourselves in this regard?

The issue is that any intense emotional state can impair clear thinking.

– *When we are disturbed by anger, our heart is not in the right place; when blinded by love, our heart is not in the right place; when overwhelmed by worries and anxieties, our heart is not in the right place; the spirit has lost its balance. (Confucius)*[229]

In such states, where emotions often cloud judgment and create the illusion that life will always remain the same, decisions may be made that one will later regret once circumstances change or the intensity of love diminishes.

Lack of control over love can lead not only to poor decisions but also to becoming a victim of abuse. Additionally, expressing affection too intensely or too quickly can push the other person away rather than draw them closer.[230]

– *Approach both women and wine with caution.*

– *Love and wine, without recklessness.*

– *Keep a cool head, even when everything else is hot.*

Incontinence and Impulsiveness

Do not be led by passion (disordered desires), lest it destroy your strength like a bull. (Sirach 6:2)[231]

At one of the vicious extremes of self-control lie incontinence and impulsiveness. Incontinence refers to the difficulty or inability to control emotional states or to refrain from doing something intensely desired, even when one knows it shouldn't be done. It also includes the inability to delay an action until the appropriate time when circumstances are more suitable.

- *Blind appetite! How many it precipitates!*
- *The force of passion leads a man to ruin. (Sirach 1:22)[232]*
- *Violent passion (disordered desires) destroys the one who harbors it and makes his enemies laugh at him. (Sirach 6:4)[233]*
- *Control your emotions, or they will control you.*

Impulsiveness is the trait of someone who often speaks or acts without reflection or caution, driven by impulses and the impression of the moment.

- *Like a city without walls, exposed to danger, is the one who cannot control their impulses. (Proverbs 25:28)[234]*
- *The fool gives full vent to his impulses, but the wise hold them back. (Proverbs 29:11)[235]*
- *Do not yield to unrefined desires, nor capitulate to every impulse.*

Both incontinence and impulsiveness can ruin promising romantic pursuits. These unpremeditated actions manifest in deviations of various self-control components, as will be discussed in the relevant topics.

Rigidity

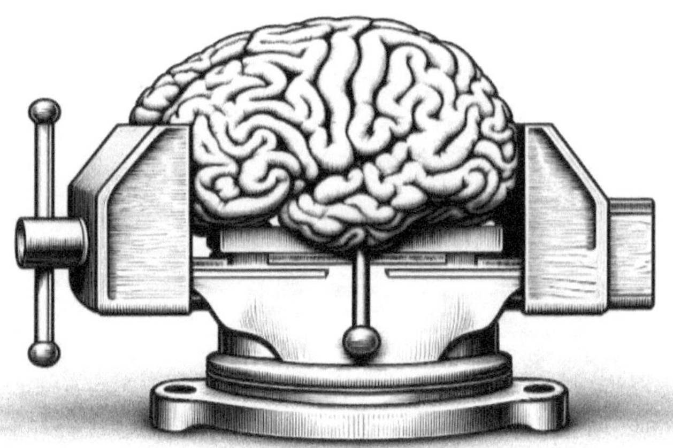

Don't be rigid; focus on results.

At the opposite extreme of self-control lies rigidity, which is characterized by difficulties or an inability to adjust decisions when necessary, leading to inflexible and unjustified self-control. This rigidity becomes an internal obstacle to fulfilling one's needs.

While circumstances align with the rigid person's limited actions, they may succeed. However, when circumstances change, their methods will no longer be effective.

—Do what is necessary at each moment. (José Martí)[236]

There are many ways to conceive and achieve a goal, so it's wise not to limit oneself to a single technique or method. As long as the rights of others and oneself are respected, any approach that yields good results can be used.

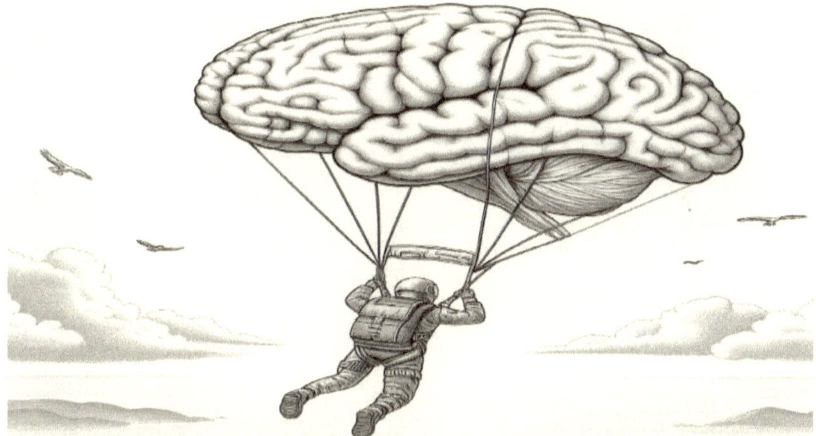

The mind and a parachute work well when they are open.

It's important to keep an open mind to other approaches that might be effective, especially when the methods currently in use are not.

—Don't fear necessary changes.

—Keep your mind occupied to achieve things; keep your mind open to understand things. (China)[237]

BOLDNESS

Who doesn't dare to cross a stream, how will they cross a lake?
(Tibet)[238]

Boldness is the ability to overcome the fear of suffering harm in a risky action.

–*Fear is conquered by daring.*

–*Without boldness, there is no glory.*

In courtship, uncertainty often outweighs certainty. Starting a romantic endeavor always carries the risk of failure. However, many times the only way to know the outcome is by taking the risk.

–*To win, you must risk.*

–*He who did not venture, neither lost nor won.*

–*If you don't dare, you won't have glory.*

–*He who does not venture does not cross the sea. (Spain)[239]*

–*He who doesn't risk an egg won't get a chicken. (Panama)[240]*

–*Where there is no risk, there is no merit.*

–*Risk sweetens the task.*

But it's not about always taking risks; it's about doing so in the right circumstances and in the way that's necessary, avoiding unnecessary risks or those whose potential unwanted consequences you're not prepared to face. After careful deliberation, the best decision might be not to take the risk. In fact, some risks aren't worth taking.

–*He who exposes himself to a useless danger dies a martyr to the devil. (Netherlands)[241]*

Boldness doesn't oppose caution or prudence; they complement each other. When taking risks, it's just as harmful to be paralyzed by inertia and fear of failure as it is to act without proper reflection.

- *Audacity without judgment is dangerous, and judgment without audacity is useless.*

Boldness as a Willingness to Advance to the Next Level

One way boldness manifests during courtship is in the readiness to move forward. If the woman is friendly and relaxed, it usually signals that you're on the right track. So, continue progressing; if conversation flows well on a walk, try to kiss her. If you're watching movies at home and start kissing, take her hand and lead her to the bedroom. Don't be afraid—if she feels uncomfortable, she'll let you know.

- *Cunning and intent, seize the moment.*

- *A bold lover is more loved by his beloved. (Spain)[242]*

- *Courage gives what beauty denies.*

- *He who is bold eats what is hidden. (Colombia)[243]*

This is about a willingness to advance, but with caution and delicacy. Remember the "iron theory" mentioned in the section on "Tact."

Impulsiveness and Recklessness

On the vicious extreme of boldness lie impulsiveness and recklessness, where one moves forward without any consideration or examination of the circumstances, ignoring the timing of love or the signals indicating the level of acceptance or rejection from the woman.

- *Acting without thinking is like shooting without aiming.*

- *Acting without thinking can make us stumble.*

Timidity

With too much shyness, you neither eat nor dine.

On the vicious extreme of deficiency lies timidity, a way of behaving in social settings characterized by unjustified and unproductive inhibitions and fears.

– To the shy and indecisive, everything seems impossible.

Courtship naturally creates tension, and if unjustified fears are added, it's unlikely to progress far.

– He who is too shy neither eats nor dines.

– Indecisive love, much flower and little fruit. (Spain)[244]

– Shyness is a sin against love.

– Cowardly loves don't reach real love.

– Don't say you have love if you lack boldness.

– A cowardly man won't conquer a beautiful woman, and if he does, a braver man will take her away.

– Platonic loves are as absurd as suicidal ones.

– A cowardly dog doesn't make love.

Although timidity isn't always a universal barrier to romantic interest, some women may distance themselves from shy men if they feel this trait hinders open communication or the development of a balanced relationship where both partners' emotional or communicative needs are met.

– A bashful lover makes the beloved suspicious.

– Love that doesn't dare is despised by women.

– Timid love is lightly regarded.

PERSEVERANCE

He who pursues it, achieves it. (Mexico)[245]

Perseverance is the steadfastness in pursuing goals despite obstacles. During courtship, perseverance is the ability to persist despite a woman's initial rejections or the challenges encountered in the pursuit of love.

- *The shell is hard, but the nut is sweet. (Spain)[246]*
- *Perseverance is the resource of the unattractive.*
- *A lover must be persistent.*
- *Drop by drop, the water carves the stone. (Spain)[247]*
- *Soft water on hard stone, with persistence, makes a hole. (Spain)[248]*
- *The drop carves the stone, not by force but by frequency.*
- *Drop by drop, the sea runs dry. (Galicia, Spain)[249]*

When the land doesn't yield, prepare to move on.

But perseverance doesn't mean persisting blindly; it means doing so intelligently—only when there are real or perceived possibilities of winning the woman over. This involves changing your approach as circumstances demand and knowing when to give up if necessary.

−*Don't waste time on what there's ample reason to believe cannot be achieved. (José Martí)[250]*

−*It's unwise to pursue what doesn't promise success. (Afro-Cuban Saying)[251]*

−*A wise farmer doesn't plow land that doesn't bear fruit. (Spain)[252]*

Law of Scarcity or Paradox of Perseverance

It's common for a man to feel that only less attractive women pursue him while those he likes reject him. This isn't coincidental but stems from his own actions and attitudes. When a man meets a highly attractive woman, the desire to win her and the fear of losing her may lead him to overwhelm her with gifts, compliments, and constant availability. This abundance can make her value him less, eventually leading to boredom and rejection because too much of anything diminishes desire.

−*The satisfied turn their back on the source.*

−*A constant delicacy dulls the appetite. (Spain)[253]*

−*We lose interest in what is certain and go crazy for what is volatile.*

−*No one cares about their shadow because it's always by their side.*

−*What I see all the time, I do not desire. (Spain)[254]*

−*No dish fails to cloy. (Spain)[255]*

–Glory every day would eventually weary. (Spain)[256]

However, when a man is not as interested in a woman, he tends to reduce his availability. This makes the woman value him more, as scarce things are more appreciated, while what is abundant is not valued in the same way.

–Scarcity raises the price. (Spain)[257]

–What is forbidden is desired.

–Prohibition excites desire, and desire makes the ugly beautiful.

–Forbidden fruit is more desired. (Spain)[258]

–Want to be loved? Make yourself desired. (Spain)[259]

–A woman's nature is to scorn what is given and long for what is denied. (Spain)[260]

–Many desire what escapes them and detest what is offered. (Ovid) [261]

This peculiar aspect of human nature works for both sexes. When a woman is always available, we feel secure and may take her for granted. Conversely, when her availability is limited, we feel uncertain and tend to value and desire her more.

The law of scarcity can also serve as a diagnostic tool in situations where a woman's interest seems tentative but unclear due to weak signals. In such cases, feigning indifference or simulating withdrawal can reveal her true feelings. If she is genuinely interested, this emotional distance may increase her interest and make it more evident.

This approach also applies when a woman has grown accustomed to our presence. By justifiably withdrawing our usual attention, she may feel and increase her emotional need for us.

–You don't know what you have until it's gone. (Afro-Cuban Saying)[262]

–A blessing is not recognized until it is lost. (Spain)[263]

It's important to clarify that while too much attention can lead to cloying and give the impression of desperation for affection or sex, too much absence can lead to being forgotten.

–He who plays at being missed risks being forgotten.

–Absence erases love. (Cuba)[264]

–The absent grow further away each day. (Japan)[265]

–Absence, the enemy of love, as far from the eyes as from the heart. (Cuba)[266]

Switching excessively between interest and indifference can give the impression of inconsistency or even mental instability, leading to rejection.

The key is to balance these behaviors according to the situation and avoid extremes.

– Virtue lies in the middle. (Latin Proverb: In medio stat virtus)[267]

– Go in the middle, and you will not fall. (Spain)[268]

– A good balance is achieved between the rein and the spur.

– Neither too much pushing that they flee, nor too much holding back that they stop. (Galicia, Spain)[269]

– Neither so cold that it freezes, nor so hot that it burns.

– Neither so high that it reaches the sky, nor so low that it crawls on the ground.

When considering the appropriate level of attention to give, it's essential to recognize that there are situations where time constraints require a more direct approach. In these cases, you may not have the luxury to gradually soften the ground with a barrage of compliments, gifts, services, or calculated indifference. Instead, with an acceptable minimum of romantic gestures and while respecting the fundamental principles of courtship, you need to get straight to the point.

Law of Scarcity and Uniqueness of Compliments in Initial Approaches

Women who stand out for their beauty are often tired of receiving compliments on their physical attributes. If you focus on this in the first interactions, you'll be just another among many who have done the same, making your approach seem unoriginal and repetitive, likely leading to rejection. As mentioned, abundance diminishes interest, and constant stimuli exhaust responses.

To spark her interest, it can be effective to behave differently from the majority who bore and irritate her. Compliment her non-physical qualities, such as her intelligence, unique character, or kind-heartedness. Alternatively, you could feign disinterest or cleverly critique her.

– Interest plays all roles, even that of disinterest.

Inconstancy

On the vicious extreme of deficiency lies inconstancy, which is the tendency to give up at the first sign of obstacles. Some women, to test the firmness of a suitor's intentions, may reject him in the initial stages. If the suitor is inconstant, he will likely be dismissed.

– Without persistence, there is no reward.

Stubbornness or Obstinacy

One must be willing to abandon false paths.

On the vicious extreme of excess lies the persistence in error, where one is unable to reassess or abandon goals or methods, even when they are clearly unwise.

- *Stubbornness is the perseverance of fools.*
- *To err is human, but to persist in error is foolish.*
- *Don't waste time banging your head against a wall hoping to turn it into a door.*

During courtship, this deviation of perseverance is evident in the inability to change approaches or to let go of a woman when necessary.

- *What has one learned from mistakes if they persist in them?*
- *The man who has made a mistake and does not correct it makes another. (Confucius)[270]*
- *If you have errors, reflect on them.*

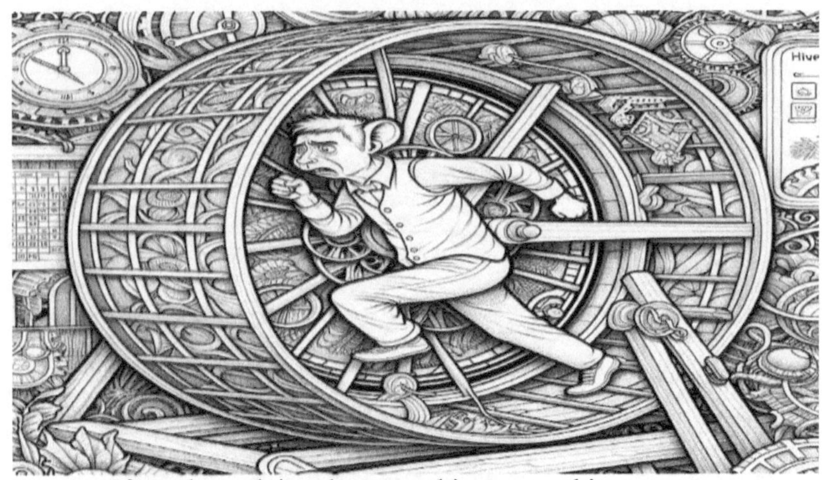

If you keep doing the same thing, everything repeats.

If you try to win a woman's love using the same methods in the same circumstances and get negative results, continuing with the same approach is likely to yield the same negative outcome.

– *It's madness to do the same thing repeatedly and expect different results.*

– *If you want different results: change.*

– *You have two choices: evolve or repeat.*

This is what happens to the stubborn and obstinate, making these traits forms of inconvenient persistence.

– *Obstinacy is a dead-end street.*

– *The obstinate ends badly.*

– *He who stubbornly insists, loses. (Afro-Cuban Saying)[271]*

Sometimes, a courtship that was progressing well can take a turn that causes significant discomfort and starts affecting other areas of life, leaving the option of giving up as a reasonable alternative.

– *What doesn't work, ruins.*

– *What's unnecessary is too much; leave it behind. (Spain)[272]*

Being an effective suitor means having the skills to find a partner, not forcing a specific person to love you. If you're within a woman's preferences, the process will likely flow smoothly.

– *In the end, when they want to, they'll come to you on their own. (Mexico)[273]*

– *In the end, when they want to, they'll give you a chance. (Mexico)[274]*

Otherwise, it's not worth persisting. Find someone for whom you are eligible, or don't let inhibitions make courtship a painful experience.

—When the land doesn't yield, prepare to move on.

—A wise farmer doesn't plow land that doesn't bear fruit. (Spain)[275]

—A business that doesn't profit should be abandoned.

—Don't seek where there's nothing. (Spain)[276]

—You won't find happiness if you look for it where it doesn't exist.

—Stagnant water doesn't move the mill. (Afro-Cuban Saying)[277]

—If something isn't progressing, let it go and move on.

How to Use a Woman's Stubbornness to Your Advantage

You can leverage a woman's stubbornness by challenging her will in various ways. Two common methods include:

Imposing sacrifices that make her value the love between both more.

—Without effort, there is no appreciation. (Mexico)[278]

—What costs little is valued little. (Spain)[279]

—We love most what we've achieved with the greatest effort.

—Quarreled loves are cherished loves.

Creating an enemy image in someone who opposes the relationship, making her willing to stand against that opposition.

PATIENCE

He who knows how to wait, achieves success.

This quality involves intelligently enduring the challenges and discomforts of a necessary wait.

- *The patient person will endure as long as necessary, and in the end, their reward will be joy. (Sirach 1:23)*[280]

- *Patience is bitter, but its fruits are sweet. (France)*[281]

- *Being patient is a sign of great intelligence; being impatient is a sign of great foolishness. (Proverbs 14:29)*[282]

- *Learn to wait wisely.*

- *Patience is the key to paradise. (Turkey)*[283]

The fruit grows slowly. (India)[284]

In courtship, patience involves enduring the discomforts that may arise and waiting wisely to enjoy the rewards.

–*Give time to the fish; it will eventually bite.*

–*The orange ripens in its own time. (Cuba)[285]*

–*The hard pear ripens with time.*

Patience and the Stages of Courtship

Every romantic pursuit is unique, unfolding in its own way. However, all share the trait of progressing through successive stages, each with its own importance. These stages may proceed at different paces, but rushing them can lead to failure.

–*To force evolution is to destroy it.*

–*The banana doesn't ripen with sticks. (India)[286]*

–*Follow the rhythms and timings of love.*

–*Do you see a tree? Do you see how long it takes for the golden orange or red pomegranate to hang from the thick branch? Well, by delving into life, you see that everything follows the same process. Love, like a tree, must go from seed to sapling, to flower, to fruit. (José Martí)[287]*

The cart doesn't go before the oxen. (Afro-Cuban Saying)[288]

It's not only important to give each stage the time it needs but also to respect the order in which they should be completed. Failing to do so can ruin everything.

- *You don't have a snack before breakfast. (Afro-Cuban Saying)[289]*
- *Don't start building the house from the roof. (Mexico)[290]*
- *Before running, one must crawl and walk. (Afro-Cuban Saying)[291]*

Familiarity breeds fondness.

On the other hand, you can't expect instant intimacy. Both must go through a period of mutual adaptation to feel comfortable and relaxed with each other's presence and behavior. If time permits, it's important to encourage this process.

–*Let her get used to your presence and interacting with you, and you with her.*

–*From looking comes loving; from not seeing comes forgetting.*

Patience and the Desire to Win Over a Woman

Many discomforts during courtship stem from an excessive desire to achieve it, which often leads to losing perspective on the necessary phases and can result in hasty actions.

–*Many of our failures come from trying to rush success.*

–*Haste is the father of failure.*

–*He who rushes, loses.*

–*Acting without thinking can make us stumble.*

The desire to win over a woman should be strong enough to make sacrifices worthwhile but not so overwhelming that it disrupts your composure.

–*If you have no desire, everything hurts. (Czechoslovakia)[292]*

–*Desire is the first law of gain.*

–*He who wants to act finds means; he who doesn't, finds excuses.*

–*He who wants to kiss finds the mouth.*

However, it shouldn't be so excessive that it disorganizes you.

–Don't rush to the chest with all your hunger, nor to the pitcher with all your thirst. (Spain)[293]

–Control your desires, or they will control you.

The discomfort from excessive desire, coupled with a lack of skill in controlling and concealing it, can project an image of desperation for affection or sex through verbal and non-verbal communication, which is highly unproductive and a significant cause of rejection.

–Desperation has never made good deals.

Opportunities and Patience

Events are like fruit; you must consume them neither a day before they ripen, nor a day after. (José Martí)[294]

If you act before circumstances are favorable, you risk being ineffective and ruining everything. Conversely, if you act after conditions have been ideal, your actions will be in vain. Patience, therefore, involves having a sense of timing, knowing when to wait for the right moment, and seizing it when it comes.

–Acting at the right time is the key to success. (Arab Proverb)[295]

–In this world, everything has its time; there is a season for everything under the sun. (Ecclesiastes 3:1-8)[296]

–The wise love finding the right moment for their actions. (Lao Tzu)[297]

–When opportunity knocks, open the door.

–Once the moment has passed, it's in vain to try to capture it.

–If you don't use the opportunity when it comes, when will you?

–Give the kite string when it hums. (Puerto Rico)[298]

—When the opportunity arrives, seize it. (Spain)[299]

You must wait for chance to create opportunities when you cannot or should not create them yourself. Otherwise, it's best to actively contribute to their formation.

—Opportunities need a little help.

—Fortune favors those who seek it. (Spain)[300]

Success comes when opportunity meets the ability to seize it, so it's also important to prepare and be diligent.

—Skill counts for little without opportunity, and opportunity counts for little without the skill to seize it.

—Chance favors the prepared mind.

—Luck is the coincidence of opportunity and the ability to seize it.

Impatience

At the vicious extreme of deficiency lies impatience, which is the inability to wait when necessary.

—Neither love, eating, nor sleeping should be rushed.

—A little impatience can ruin great plans. (China)[301]

—He who lacks patience lacks everything. (Italy)[302]

Passivity, Stubbornness, or Obstinacy

The excessive extremes include passivity, where one tolerates unfavorable circumstances or irritating traits without being obliged to.

—It's better to blush once than to pale twenty times.

Or the stubbornness of waiting for something despite its senselessness.

—Stubbornness leads nowhere. (Afro-Cuban Saying)[303]

—Persistence often results in loss. (Afro-Cuban Saying)[304]

—Whimsy produces loss. (Afro-Cuban Saying)[305]

—The stubborn will endure much suffering. (Sirach 3:27)[306]

Patience doesn't mean waiting indefinitely, enduring all discomforts, or investing endless resources. It's wise to set limits, and once they are crossed, it's prudent to retreat.

—One must know when to retreat. (Mexico)[307]

—Retreating in time is a sign of discretion. (Spain)[308]

—A timely retreat is itself a victory. (Spain)[309]

—Sometimes we must let go, not because we don't care, but because they don't.

–Don't seek where there's nothing. (Spain)[310]

–You can't take from where there's nothing.

Promptness

From skilled to skilled, the fastest wins. (Spain)[311]

This quality involves doing or saying something with promptness, diligence, and brevity when circumstances demand it.

–Promptness is the mother of good fortune.

–The early bird gets the worm. (Panama)[312]

–Whoever arrives early grinds early.

–First come, first served.

–He who gets wet early has time to dry off.

–The one at the back gets bitten by the dog.

In competition, especially in courtship, where you often compete with others for a woman's love, being the first to act is a great advantage.

–He who strikes first, strikes twice, for the blow he dealt and for getting ahead of the others.

It's important to note that patience and promptness complement each other. Patience involves knowing when to wait, but also acting quickly and diligently when needed. Promptness involves acting swiftly, but knowing when to pause.

Acting or speaking quickly without consideration can be harmful; waiting without action when the time is right, is equally unproductive.

–Patience without diligence is a poor virtue and empty knowledge.

There's a time to go slow and a time to go fast.

Considering the stages of courtship doesn't mean always moving slowly. To succeed, it's essential to assess the situation's characteristics and act quickly or slowly as needed.

–*Going fast has its advantages, going slow has its advantages. (African Proverb)*[313]

Tardiness and Laziness

At the vicious extreme of this quality lie tardiness and laziness, where one fails to act at the right moment, thereby missing valuable opportunities.

–*Don't put off for tomorrow what you should do today.*

–*What is delayed stays delayed.*

–*The street of "later" leads to the square of "never." (Colombia)*[314]

–*"Later" has no end.*

–*The lazy person says "tomorrow," but it never comes. (Afro-Cuban Saying)*[315]

As the lazy and slow act without enthusiasm, they remain stuck in desire.

–*The desire of the lazy kills him, for his hands refuse to work; all day long, he craves. (Proverbs 21:25-26)*[316]

–*The lazy do not plow in season; at harvest time they look but find nothing. (Proverbs 20:4)*[317]

–*Laziness brings deep sleep, and the idle will suffer hunger. (Proverbs 19:15)*[318]

Every victory requires well-directed efforts, without which it is impossible to succeed, and romantic conquest is no exception.

−He who waits for fruit to fall into his mouth will have little happiness.

−He who waits for luck should sit down. (Afro-Cuban Saying)[319]

−A dog that doesn't walk doesn't find a bone. (Afro-Cuban Saying)[320]

−A sleeping fox doesn't find a chicken in its belly at dawn. (Spain)[321]

−A sleeping cat doesn't catch mice. (Mexico)[322]

−The lying wolf catches no prey, nor does the sleeping man gain victory.[323]

Haste

Acting Without Thinking Is Like Shooting Without Aiming.

At the opposite vicious extreme of excess lies haste, where one rushes into actions or words without consideration or prudence.

−Acting without thinking is like shooting without aiming.

−Haste is the father of failure.

−Quick and well almost never go together.

−Excessive speed exposes us to errors.

−Business done in haste is bad business.

−Zeal without reflection is not good; too much haste causes mistakes. (Proverbs 19:2)[324]

−He who hastens delays or loses.

Marrying poorly and regretting it go hand in hand. (Spain)[325]

The inconsideration and imprudence that accompany haste can lead to trying to marry someone with whom there is no compatibility or who possesses negative qualities that could later cause significant suffering.

−Those who marry poorly always weep. (Spain)[326]

−Nothing is heavier than a poorly managed marriage.

−Beauty without prudence brings strife to the husband.

One way patience manifests in courtship is by taking the necessary time to evaluate the other person's qualities and the compatibility between both, as negative aspects could be reasons to halt further actions.[327]

−Better to walk than ride a bad horse.

−Better to be single than poorly married. (Spain)[328]

−Better alone than in bad company. (Cuba)[329]

EQUANIMITY

Equanimity is the ability to remain stable and not lose composure in the face of undesired outcomes or success.

−In prosperity, be prudent; in adversity, be patient. (Netherlands)[330]

−Neither exalt yourself for wealth nor abase yourself for poverty.

−In prosperity, be cautious; in adversity, be patient. (Portugal)[331]

−In times of good fortune or adversity, you see... whether a person has a great or small mind. (China)[332]

−He who deliberates in moments of fear or joy, and does not act hastily, will have no regrets. (Panchatantra)[333]

"Slump" or "Bad Streak"

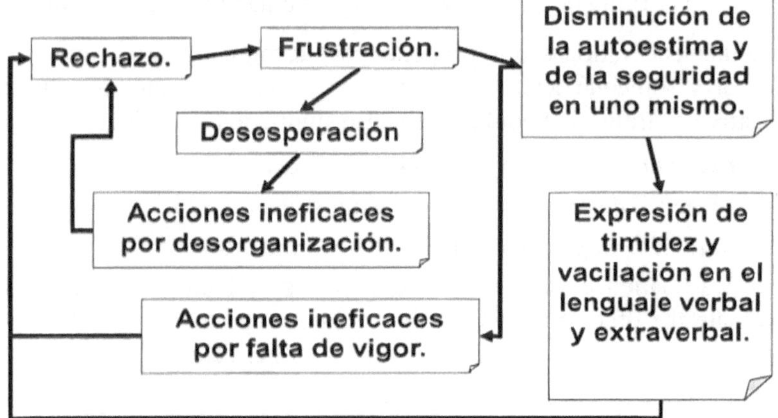

Mechanism of Psychological Slump or "Bad Streak"

A psychological slump or "bad streak" is a form of disorganization in response to undesired outcomes. It is characterized by a state of collapse and psychological disarray, where one feels that nothing goes right despite all efforts.

−The eyes strain, the feet tire, the hands cannot reach. (Spain)[334]

−To toil and toil, and achieve little or nothing; this is a common complaint.

The frustration generated by this state leads to desperation, which in turn causes disorganized and hasty actions that lead to rejection.

−Desperation remedies nothing.

−If you lose your head in difficult situations, you will only make things worse.

−He who rushes loses.

Verbal and nonverbal expressions of desperation to find a partner are themselves a cause of rejection.

—Neither with all your hunger to the chest, nor with all your thirst to the jug. (Spain)[335]

Frustration also leads to a decrease in self-esteem and self-confidence, which manifests in verbal and nonverbal communication as shyness and hesitation, inviting rejection.

—He who asks timidly invites denial.

Lowered self-esteem also results in ineffective actions due to hesitation and lack of the necessary vigor to achieve the desired effect.

—Much hesitation, little success.

—While doubt stands between desire and the desired object, it acts as a barrier, making it difficult to reach.

In this state, mental confusion occurs, making it difficult or impossible to think clearly or reflect on and correct mistakes.

—Turbid water does not make a mirror. (Spain)[336]

Additionally, women tend to reject men whom they know have been rejected by others, contributing to the slump.

All of the above creates a vicious cycle of failure, frustration, lowered self-esteem, insecurity, desperation, and verbal and non-verbal expressions of urgency in finding a partner. This leads to disorganized, hesitant, and ineffective actions, along with difficulties in reflecting on and correcting mistakes, which in turn generates more failures and frustration, perpetuating the cycle.

In such circumstances, it is advisable to stop your actions, mentally distance yourself from the situation, and take some time to focus on other matters.

—Some goals are like butterflies; when you eagerly chase after them, they stay out of reach, but if you sit quietly and calmly, they may land on you.

The full cat plays with the mouse.

Just as there can be psychological disarray and collapse rooted in frustration from real or imagined rejections, there is also the opposite state of strengthening and organization based on highly valued successes. This leads to feeling confident, relaxed, and free from any sense of urgency.

– *When the cat is full, it plays with the mouse. (Latin Proverb: Catus saepe satur cum capto mure jocatur)*[337]

Being relaxed allows for greater perception of a woman's sexual signals, which may objectively increase due to one's own relaxed behavior and expressions of self-confidence, further fueled by the curiosity of women who know he attracts others.

Perceiving an increase in demand boosts self-esteem and confidence, creating a positive, albeit temporary, cycle of psychological strengthening and organization, commonly referred to as a "good streak."

The Transient Nature of Success and Failure

It never rained without clearing, nor cleared without raining.[338]

It's human nature to believe that life will always be as successful or as unsuccessful as it feels in the current moment. However, the circumstances that define both success and failure, as well as our perceptions of them, are always changing, making both inherently temporary. This applies to courtship and the so-called "good" and "bad" streaks as well.[339]

– *Joy and anger, happiness and sorrow, worries and pains, indecisions and fears, come to us in turns, in ever-changing forms. (Chuang Tzu)[340]*

– *...The wise man... examines fullness and decline; therefore, he does not rejoice in success nor grieve in failure, knowing that conditions are not constant. (Chuang Tzu)[341]*

– *Being happy with success and unhappy with failure means being a child of circumstances; how can such a person be called self-possessed? (China)[342]*

Impulsivity and Incontinence

At the vicious extreme of deficiency lie impulsivity and incontinence, which have already been discussed at the beginning of this topic as vices of self-control.

Impassiveness

At the vicious extreme of excess is impassiveness, where one remains indifferent to situations that warrant interest and attention.

RESIGNATION

This quality involves accepting and being at peace with situations where nothing can be done to change them, or where action is possible but not advisable.

−Accept what cannot be changed.

However, resignation is not merely acceptance; it degenerates into passivity if one does not change what can and should be changed.

−Change the things that must be changed. (Latin Phrase: Mutatis mutandis)[343]

Resignation as Acceptance of Being Rejected as a Couple

Resignation in courtship manifests in several ways. One is accepting the reality that, just as not all women are attractive to you, you are not attractive to all women, and for some, you may be dismissible as a potential couple.

−No one is a treat for everyone to like.

Non-reciprocity and even rejection should be accepted with calmness, without resentment or aggressive behavior.

−Anything done out of spite is poorly done.

−You can never win a heart by force.

−Water you won't drink, let it flow. (Spain)[344]

Just as we have the right not to reciprocate someone else's love, others have the right not to reciprocate ours.

−Love that isn't returned, let it be.

−Loving without being loved is time poorly spent. (Spain)[345]

−Loving without being loved is love and time wasted. (Mexico)[346]

−Loving is time wasted if it's not reciprocated. (Spain)[347]

There are more people in the world; a rejection or failed attempt is not the end. When nothing works out, it's important to know when to walk away and start a new project.

−One nail drives out another. (Spain)[348]

−The king is dead, long live the king. (Spain)[349]

−A dead soldier is replaced by another. (Spain)[350]

−For loves that fade, seek loves that come near. (Mexico)[351]

Love and wind: for every one that goes, hundreds come. (Spain)[352]

Don't waste time or effort on people for whom you're outside their range of interest. Within the group of women who attract us, there will surely be some for whom we are good candidates as a couple or for any type of romantic relationship. The key is finding that match.

- *In the kingdom of love, some love and others are loved; happiness is being able to be both. (Afro-Cuban Saying)[353]*
- *For love to work, it must be reciprocal.*
- *True love is a two-way street.*

Resignation as the Ability to Accept One's Own Mistakes

It's no use crying over spilled milk. (England)[354]

Resignation also involves accepting when a promising courtship has gone awry.

- *What happened cannot be undone.*
- *Face up to what's done. (Spain)[355]*
- *What's done is done. (Afro-Cuban Saying)[356]*

View mistakes as unsatisfactory methods and failures as undesired outcomes from which valuable lessons can be learned.

- *Lessons come from hard knocks. (Afro-Cuban Saying)[357]*
- *He who doesn't fall, doesn't get up. (Spain)[358]*
- *If you don't fail, you don't learn; if you don't learn, you don't change; and if you don't change, you don't grow.*
- *Learning from your own mistakes is called experience.*

Resignation as the Ability to Accept Breakups

Another way resignation manifests during courtship is in accepting with dignity the loss of a woman's love when the relationship ends with no chance of reconciliation. When faced with irreparable situations or irreversible losses, the only option is to accept them and rebuild your life.

- *What can't be fixed, forgetting is best. (Spain)[359]*
- *Knowing how to endure makes suffering easier.*
- *Winners save time and pain.*
- *Knowing how to lose is a way of winning.*

—When something can't be fixed, the best approach is to endure it. (Seneca)[360]

Sometimes, an individual finds it so difficult to overcome the loss of a love that they make it the center of their existence. This not only prolongs their suffering unnecessarily but also makes it difficult to rebuild their life according to their new reality.

—Clinging to the past is a way of living in it, preventing progress into the future.

—If you don't let go of the past, how will you grab hold of the future?

—In any circumstance, remember that life goes on.

—Life changes, but it doesn't stop.

—Tears obscure the path ahead. (India)[361]

—He who doesn't look ahead, stays behind. (Spain)[362]

—Look forward so you don't fall behind. (Benjamin Franklin)[363]

—Not progressing is falling back. (Latin Phrase: Non progredi est regredi)[364]

—We must anticipate and move with the world. Glory belongs to those who look forward, not back. (José Martí)[365]

Conformism and Passivity

One of the vicious extremes of resignation is conformism, which involves accepting and being content with situations or conditions that one can and should change for the better.

Nonconformity and Complaining

At the other extreme is nonconformity, characterized by hostility toward established political, social, moral, or aesthetic orders.

—Nothing satisfies the discontented. (Cuba)[366]

—It's a bad ailment to never be content.

—If given gold earrings, the discontented will complain they're heavy. (Cuba)[367]

Complaining, frequent and habitual, often lacks a solid reason.

—If you cry at night for the absence of the sun, you won't see the stars.

Both traits make the company of those who possess them unpleasant, which is a disadvantage in courtship.

FINAL CONSIDERATIONS

Since courtship and relationships are delicate matters, an essential quality for successful romance is self-control. In summary:

- Self-control is the ability to overcome inclinations or aversions when necessary.

- At one end of self-control is impulsiveness and lack of restraint, while at the other is rigidity in adapting behavior or approach when needed.

- Components of self-control include:
  o **Boldness**: The ability to overcome the fear of suffering harm (or failing in a risky action) in the circumstances and in the way that it's necessary.
  o **Patience**: The ability to endure the discomfort of a necessary wait.
  o **Promptness**: The skill to speak or act quickly, diligently, and briefly when circumstances require it.
  o **Perseverance**: The firmness in purpose despite internal and external obstacles.
  o **Equanimity**: The ability to remain stable and not become disorganized when facing unwanted results or even success.
  o **Resignation**: Acceptance of situations where nothing can be done to remedy them, or where something can be done, but shouldn't be.

- Self-control and its components enable you to regulate your personality appropriately during courtship, and even allow you to pause or withdraw if necessary.

- A lack of self-control in matters of love can lead to poor decisions, making the uncontrolled person a victim of abuse or causing them to become aggressive. Additionally, expressing affection too intensely or too quickly, instead of attracting, tends to repel the other person.

With the moral qualities analyzed in previous chapters, you can be effective in courtship, but only if they are used in coordination. Therefore, it's beneficial to reflect on the relationship between these qualities. It's also important to consider the responsibility we have towards sex and eroticism, the place they should hold in our lives, and the approach to courtship after achieving a romantic conquest that we wish to maintain.

~~~

Chapter 6. FINAL REFLECTIONS ON CONQUEST

This chapter will explore how the previously discussed qualities interrelate and offer suggestions on the appropriate place of sexuality in a person's life.

Relationship Between the Moral Qualities Analyzed

There is a close interrelationship among the four groups of moral qualities analyzed, and all are necessary for courtship to be of high quality and effective.

The prudence needed for correctly choosing whom to court provides guidance, helping to determine which individuals are worth pursuing and which should be avoided, thereby steering one toward relationships that are worthwhile.

The qualities required to detect and interpret a woman's sexual signals and weaknesses also offer guidance by helping to assess the potential for forming a romantic relationship with her.

However, orientation alone is not enough. Action is required to progress, and this is where self-control and its various components—boldness, perseverance, patience, equanimity, and resignation—come into play.

–Act to conquer.

–Bold action often leads to victory. (Spain)[368]

–Without daring, there is no glory.

Being well-positioned and taking action is still not sufficient, as attracting a woman requires delicate social skills. Therefore, urbanity, with its corresponding components—courtesy, tact, refined praise, generosity, discretion, decorum, self-confidence, and a sense of humor—among others, is crucial for relating appropriately to others.

Only with urbanity and self-control, but without the qualities needed to detect and interpret a woman's sexual signals, would one be acting blindly. Yet, having perceptiveness without urbanity and self-control would also hinder progress.

–Strength without skill breaks much; skill without strength achieves little.

Having the qualities necessary for effective courtship but lacking the prudence to choose the right person to court or reject could lead to relationships that later cause avoidable problems.

Necessary Warnings

Everything has its place, time, and measure.

This work has presented social skills and resources that can enhance effectiveness in courtship, thereby increasing the impact of one's actions.

   –Knowledge is power.

   –What others call luck, I call knowledge. (Spain)[369]

However, all power and freedom come with the responsibility to avoid unjustly harming others or oneself due to rash actions.

   –Careful planning leads to success; hasty actions lead to ruin. (Proverbs: 21:5)[370]

On the other hand, when the pursuit of romantic partners is prioritized improperly and conducted chaotically, it can lead to the neglect of other important areas of life, ultimately impoverishing one's existence.

   –He who acts without measure is destined for bankruptcy.

   –What exceeds the limit of moderation rests on an unstable point. (Seneca)[371]

If courtship and sexual pleasures are prioritized above all else and at all times, one is at risk of becoming addicted to sex and falling into the moral vice of lust.

   –He who is a slave to his body is not truly free. (Seneca)[372]

   –If you lack inner freedom, what other freedom can you hope for?[373]

   –He who does not possess himself is extremely poor.

This condition leads to countless negative consequences.

   –Vice is a precipice.

−Vice carves its own punishment.

−Many of our sufferings stem from some vice.

−Feeding a vice costs more than raising two children. (Spain)[374]

Romantic conquest and eroticism have their place, time, and measure. They should enrich and beautify life, not become the center of it to the point of enslavement.

−Sex is for the human being, not the human being for sex.

After the Conquest

To weapons, women, and books, attention must be paid every day. (Holland)[375]

Does courtship end with romantic conquest? Certainly not. If your efforts have led to a stable relationship that you wish to maintain, it's crucial to continue nurturing it. This ongoing attention helps prevent the ever-present threat of external romantic interest from succeeding.

−Orchards, mills, and women require constant use. (Spain)[376]

−Plants, women, and knowledge need care to thrive.

−A mill that doesn't grind falls into ruin.

José Martí beautifully emphasized the importance of persistence in courtship:

−Love is a fierce creature that needs new nourishment every day. (José Martí)[377]

−Love is greedy, insatiable, active; it does not rest content with past sacrifices but thrives on current ones. It is a restless force that requires daily sustenance, a desire that is never fully satisfied. It's not merely

physical satisfaction it craves; only continual, tender, visible, and tangible attentions nourish it. (José Martí)[378]

–*The loving attentions we give form a resistance within the soul of the beloved against the invasion of outside love. (José Martí)*[379]

–*Tenderness is a perpetual work, a task of every moment. Otherwise, unfulfilled love will seek fulfillment elsewhere! One word sums up the entire strategy of love: dew-drop. There should always be a pearl on the green leaf—a word whispered in the ear, a glance that sways in our eyes, a moist kiss on the forehead. He who loves this way will never be unloved. He will fall and rise again, crying in despair, lost in black abysses, and die alone. (José Martí)*[380]

FINAL CONSIDERATIONS

Everything in excess is harmful, even sexuality and love. That is why this chapter calls for keeping these important areas of existence in their rightful place. In summary:

- There is a close interrelationship among the four groups of moral qualities analyzed, and all are necessary for courtship to be of quality and effective. It is as important to know how to choose correctly whom to court and whom to reject, as it is to interpret a woman's sexual signals and weaknesses, to know when to advance, pause, or even retreat when necessary, and to have the social subtleties required for appropriate social interaction.

- Romantic conquest, sex, and eroticism have their place, time, and measure. These should serve to enrich and make life more beautiful and fulfilling, not to live entirely for them.

- It is advisable to always maintain, to some extent, the initiatives that led to a stable relationship that one wishes to preserve. This helps prevent the ever-present threat of external romantic interest from taking root.

This proposal for reflection on courtship and the importance of moral qualities to be effective in it while remaining responsible concludes here.

Solutions have been presented that sometimes surprise with their simplicity, and readers may realize that much of the knowledge presented here was already within them before reading this book, albeit in a disorganized and disconnected manner, making it difficult to apply at the appropriate time. Let this text serve as a source of ideas or as an organizer of what was already known. If it helps someone make their life more interesting, the author will be more than satisfied.

~~

GENERAL TIPS FOR SEDUCING WISELY

This section provides a concise overview of the ideas presented throughout the work, each of which is encapsulated by the charm of a proverb. Among the wise tips for winning hearts, the following can be mentioned:

1. **Talk About Topics of Interest to Her:** You can attract a woman sexually by subtly expressing your romantic intentions and tuning in with her. This is achieved by listening and asking questions, encouraging her to talk about herself, and focusing on topics that interest her more than what interests you. - He who knows how to listen, knows how to speak.

2. **Take Care of Your Appearance and Personal Image:** While personal appearance isn't everything, it plays a significant role in sexual attraction. Women often consciously or unconsciously associate a man's external appearance with the quality of his inner world and his potential to meet their personal tastes and the needs of a future family. - Good appearance is a letter of recommendation and credibility.

3. **Choose appropriate places for courting.** The best circumstances for courtship are those that facilitate communication and allow both parties to feel comfortable with the environment and each other's presence. Choosing these well increases the chances that everything will flow smoothly and be defined without many setbacks; whereas, with a poor choice, the opposite usually happens. - The quality of circumstances for courting is like that of the soil and climate for the farmer who plants.

4. **Approach the lady away from her group of friends.** Due to the internal dynamics of groups and the pressures they exert on their members, both the lady and the gentleman usually feel observed and uncomfortable when courting or being courted under this influence. This constitutes an obstacle to mutual closeness, so it is advantageous to isolate from them. - Divide and conquer.

5. **Initiate the first moves while avoiding being noticed by the group members.** If it is not possible to physically isolate, it is advisable to conceal intentions and initial actions from the group members. - Discretion is one of the secrets to success.

6. **Plan the reconnection.** When talking to a woman you are attracted to, but there is a possibility of not seeing her again and therefore not communicating anymore, find ways to reconnect with her, such as getting her phone number, email, social media, place of study or work, etc. - Without communication, there can be no courtship.

7. **Visit places frequented by women with the characteristics you are interested in.** Depending on the characteristics of the places, so will be

the characteristics of the women who frequent them. Therefore, depending on the type of woman you want as a partner, you should frequent such places. - To catch fish, go to the river.

8. **It's not necessary to be extraordinarily handsome or wealthy to find a partner.** While physical attractiveness and economic status are important during courtship, they are just some of the many variables a woman considers. With normal resources, and even compensating for the lack or absence of some with the abundance of others, victory can still be achieved. - You will fight and win by using your resources wisely.

9. **Don't feel pressured to succeed, nor ashamed of your unsuccessful attempts.** While a high number of unsuccessful attempts may require revisiting your courtship techniques, no one is successful all the time. - You can't play and never lose.

10. **Don't fear beautiful women.** Very beautiful women are often very lonely because no one dares to court them. Because of this, the chances of the one who does court them can be high. - Fortune favors the bold. (Virgil)[381]

11. **Don't look for the perfect woman, because she doesn't exist.** If your selection and exclusion criteria are extraordinarily high, it's possible that no woman in the world will be able to meet them, which, far from helping, will prevent you from finding a partner, as all will be dismissible. - He who wants a mule without blemish, let him walk on foot. (Spain)[382]

12. **Choose wisely whom to court or reject.** If you lack selection and exclusion criteria, or if they are flawed, you may establish relationships that will later cause many problems that could have been avoided. - If love doesn't suit you, let someone else have it.

13. **Be perceptive of the sexual signals a woman emits.** Proceeding without regard for the signals from the woman that indicate the extent to which you are accepted or rejected means acting blindly. - With your eyes closed, you can't move forward. (Afro-Cuban proverb)[383]

14. **Learn to listen to yourself.** It's important to pay attention to what you feel about the woman and the relationship with her overall since a very important element, and sometimes the only one necessary to decide not to start or to stop a courtship, is simply not feeling good. - To orient yourself, become aware.

15. **Study the woman and position yourself in her.** Weak points are entry points to a woman's heart, so it's advisable to know them and work on them with words and temptations. - Strike where there is a need.

16. **Know your best assets and use them wisely.** If your strengths or best resources align with the woman's weak points, the chances of success can be high, so it's worth becoming aware of these and learning to use them. - Self-knowledge is the foundation of all wisdom.

17. **Learn to put yourself in the woman's perspective.** If there is one quality that is important for achieving success in life in general and in courtship in particular, it is the ability to put yourself in others' shoes. - If you're not able to put yourself in someone else's place, you won't get far.

18. **Be realistic.** Avoid letting your feelings prevent you from seeing reality as it truly is, so that you don't invent baseless hopes. - Mirages are not reality. (Afro-Cuban proverb)[384]

19. **Be affable, but with limits.** Learn to have good manners, but make it clear that there are limits regarding the type of treatment you're willing to endure and what you're willing to do to win or keep her love. - Humility and fierceness, all in one piece.

20. **Make progressive advances and withdrawals to study the woman's reaction.** One way to understand a woman's disposition toward your courtship is by making gradual advances and withdrawals, observing her response each time. If her reactions show that you are well accepted, you can progressively increase the level of conversation and physical contact. However, if they show discomfort or rejection, it's a sign of where the boundary lies, and you should avoid further advances for the time being. - The careful foot goes where it pleases. (China)[385]

21. **Respect personal space.** When you first talk to a woman, avoid getting so close that you make her feel uncomfortable. - Even among the trees in the forest, there's space.

22. **Learn to appreciate women's good qualities.** A well-timed and clever compliment may not lead to a romantic relationship, but at the very least, it will be well received. - Tell her she's beautiful, and you'll have put a sweet in her mouth.

23. **Compliment her and study her reactions.** Sometimes a woman doesn't spontaneously show signs of acceptance or rejection, or these signs are very subtle. One way to understand her disposition to being courted is by complimenting her qualities and observing her reactions. In this sense, compliments serve a diagnostic function. If the signals are positive, you can gradually increase the intensity of compliments and other expressions of interest until reaching physical contact. In this other sense, they serve a therapeutic function. - A sweet mouth opens an iron door. (Sephardic Jewish proverb)[386]

24. **Keep a cool head, even if everything else is heated.** Expressing feelings of love too much or too quickly doesn't attract the other person; it scares them away. - With women and wine, don't lose your mind.

25. **Give unexpected gestures, but don't overwhelm her with gifts.** An untimely, overly expensive, or extravagant gift doesn't make a woman feel special and unique; it overwhelms her and generates confusion and distrust. This can cause her to distance herself, or she may keep an emotional distance to continue receiving gifts, fearing they will stop once she's won over. - Be romantic, but not foolishly romantic.

26. **Move slowly or quickly depending on the circumstances.** It's important to consider the occasion's characteristics and move fast or slow as they require. - There are times to move slowly and others to move quickly.

27. **Be direct when necessary.** Sometimes, due to limited time, you can't wait for a bombardment of attention or indifference to soften the ground. Instead, with a minimum acceptable level of romance and respecting the most basic principles of courtship, you must get straight to the point. - If time is tight, don't beat around the bush.

28. **Avoid talking about your romantic conquests.** Generally, women care about their reputation and avoid illicit relationships due to the possible social consequences. If they find out that a man habitually discusses his conquests and brags about his "feats," they will know that being involved with him could have bad consequences, which is a significant reason to reject him. - A hawk that hunts women doesn't wear bells.

29. 10- **Keep your plans to yourself.** If you share your interest in a woman with other potential competitors, you may inadvertently spark their interest, causing them to move ahead. - The art of silence is as great as the art of speech. (Germany)[387]

30. **Use others' lack of discretion to your advantage.** If someone shows interest in a woman you're interested in, you might lessen his affection by criticizing his taste and giving negative evaluations of the woman's beauty. - The fish dies by the mouth. (Spain)[388]

31. **Be mindful of who advises you.** Be careful when seeking advice on love matters because the advisor might have interests contrary to yours and make suggestions that could harm you. - Some give advice for their own benefit.

32. **Respect yourself.** If a woman rejects you and even mistreats you in her refusal, yet you continue to insist, what you generate is contempt. - You can't love someone you don't respect.

33. **Have a sense of humor.** A genuine sense of humor makes the company of the person who has it entertaining and denotes intelligence and good mental and physical health, characteristics highly valued, both consciously and unconsciously, by the opposite sex. - A sense of humor is almost an aphrodisiac.

34. **Be bold, and without rushing, try to move to the next level.** If you advance with the right technique and the woman feels uncomfortable, she will let you know, at which point you should stop; but if her responses indicate that she feels comfortable and that you are well received, you have the green light to try to move to the next level. - A bold suitor is preferred by the ladies.

35. **Follow the rhythms and timing of love.** Every stage in the journey toward a romantic relationship has its role, so it is important to avoid rushing through them if you want to succeed. - Forcing the natural evolution is to destroy it.

36. **Encourage her to get used to your presence and interacting with you.** Instant intimacy cannot be expected; both must go through a period of mutual adaptation to feel comfortable and relaxed in each other's presence. If time allows, it's important to encourage this to happen. - Familiarity breeds affection.

37. **Avoid projecting the image of someone desperate for love or sex.** The discomfort caused by excessive desire to win a woman over, combined with a lack of skill in controlling and concealing it, can project the image of someone desperate for love or sex, which is a significant cause of rejection. - Desperation in business leads to bad deals.

38. **Act at the right moment.** If you act before circumstances are favorable, you will be ineffective and may ruin everything; if you act after the right moment, your efforts will be in vain. - Everything in its time. (Czech saying))[389]

39. **Set limits on the amount of resources to use.** Set boundaries regarding the time, effort, and other resources you're willing to invest in a romantic pursuit; once those limits are reached, withdraw from the battle that demands more than you're willing to give. - A glorious retreat is as honorable as a brave charge.

40. **Learn to persist intelligently.** Persist when you perceive possibilities, but change your approach as circumstances require. There is a time to try and a time to give up. (Ecclesiastes: 3,6)[390]

41. **Don't persist in error.** If you try to win a woman's love through certain methods, under certain circumstances, and get negative results, but you

continue to pursue her under the same circumstances and with the same methods, you're likely to keep getting the same negative results. - If you want different results, don't do the same thing over and over.

42. **Avoid being available 100% of the time.** When you meet a woman who is very attractive to you, the desire to have her and the fear of losing her may lead you to shower her with gifts, compliments, and services, and be available to her all the time, which can make her appreciate you less until she gets bored and rejects you, because abundance kills desire and constant stimulation exhausts the response. - Abundance brings boredom. (Spain)[391]

43. **Learn to show indifference when necessary.** If you pretend some indifference or feign a withdrawal when you sense that the woman is starting to take an interest in you, that emotional distancing generally unsettles her and causes concern about what she did, said, or lacks to make this happen. This tends to increase her interest and makes it more evident. - Deprivation leads to appetite.

44. **Properly dose the changes in approach.** Changing from showing interest to indifference too excessively or inappropriately can give the impression of being fickle or having some sort of mental disorder, leading to rejection. The key is to dose these changes properly according to the demands of the circumstances and avoid excesses. - Going too far is just as bad as falling short. (Cuba)[392]

45. **Avoid cliché compliments in the first approaches.** Women who stand out for their physical beauty are usually tired of receiving compliments about it, so if that's exactly what you praise in your first approach, you'll be just one among many who do so daily. Since your way of courting her is so unspectacular, repetitive, and worn out for her, it's likely to cause rejection. - To the full blackbird, all cherries are bitter. (Germany)[393]

46. **Use the woman's stubbornness to your advantage.** A woman's stubbornness can be stimulated and used to your advantage through methods such as finding an enemy in someone who opposes the love between you, whom she would be willing to defy, and imposing sacrifices in relation to that romantic bond that make her value it more. - Want someone to stay strongly tied to you? Impose great sacrifices on them.

47. **During a slump or "bad streak," stop your actions and focus on other activities for a while.** When you feel that nothing is working with anyone despite all your efforts, stop your actions, mentally distance yourself from the situation, and take some time to focus on other matters.

- If you chase after butterflies, they fly away, but if you stay calm and silent, they might land on you.

48. **Adjust your expectations.** Accept the reality that just as not all women are attractive to you, you are not attractive to all women, and some may reject you. - No one can be liked by everyone.

49. **Accept unrequited love with serenity.** Unreciprocated love, and even rejection, should be accepted with serenity and should not lead to any resentment, much less aggressive behavior. - Let go of what cannot be or is not meant for you.

50. **Learn from mistakes.** View mistakes as unsatisfactory procedures and failures as undesired outcomes from which you can always gain experience. - Falls make riders. (Mexico)[394]

51. **Accept irreparable romantic breakups with dignity.** When a relationship ends with no possibility of reconciliation, it is important to accept the woman's loss of love with dignity and rebuild your life based on the new situation. - Where there is no remedy, there must be resignation.

52. **Even after establishing the relationship, continue to be attentive and thoughtful.** It is important that the initiatives that resulted in a stable relationship you wish to maintain continue to some extent. This helps prevent the ever-present threat of outside love interests. - He who has a shop should take care of it, or sell it. (Cuba)[395]

53. **Avoid neglecting other important areas of your life by being too focused on courtship.** Romantic pursuit and eroticism, when placed in the right context, time, and measure, serve to make life more beautiful and fulfilling, but prioritizing them at all times brings bad consequences. - For a prosperous life: art, order, and moderation. (Spain)[396]

~~~

COMPLIMENTS

A compliment should be brief and understandable.

A compliment is a witty, clever, original, and timely phrase used to celebrate feminine beauty. It's a form of verbal artistry and should never be crude. It's a refined form of flattery and must highlight qualities that the lady truly possesses; otherwise, it could come across as mocking and lead to rejection. The compliment should be understandable, typically short, and delivered in a seductive tone.

It's important to note that each culture has its own perspective on these, and in some, they may not be well-received.

Below are examples of compliments, organized according to the element used as a reference to compliment the woman.[397]

Food-Inspired Compliments

Almost like a declaration that feminine beauty and charm are as delightful as the tastiest dish or true nourishment for the soul, many compliments compare women to food and the pleasures they bring.

–*A year without eating, and just seeing you keeps me alive.*

–*Tell me your diet so my girlfriend can follow it.*

–*If you cook like you walk, I'll even eat the crumbs.*

–*You're so sweet, just looking at you makes me gain weight.*

–*Don't walk in the sun, you'll melt, sweetie!*

–*Ma'am, thank God I'm diabetic because your daughter is a sweet treat, and if I taste her, I'd die.*

–*You dropped a wrapper. - Which one? - The one that wraps you, sweetie.*

−Gentlemen, if sweets could walk!

−Hey, sweetie, I love chocolate.

−I wish I were a guava candy, so you could eat me with that sweet mouth.

−Your mom must be a pastry chef because a treat like you doesn't come from just anyone.

−Please walk in the shade; the sun melts sweet treats.

−If you were chocolate, I'd love to be the first to taste you...

−Look at that treat, and here I am with diabetes!

−How I wish I were candy to stick to your lips and melt in your mouth!

−My love, you have so much meat, and I have no teeth.

−Your father must be a butcher because you got all the prime cuts.

−And they say there's no meat. What's missing are cans to pack it in.

−So much meat, and I'm starving.

−With the sauce you've got and the fool that I am, what a fricassee we'd make.

−Goodbye, jelly!

Anatomical Compliments

These compliments refer to the beauty of the female anatomy or to some part of the male anatomy that suffers from her absence or is overwhelmed by her beauty. To avoid being crude, it's important to carefully choose which body part is used as an expressive resource.

−You have a mouth that is a sigh.

−You have a mouth that is a dream.

−I need my heart to live, but I need you more because you make it beat.

−Those beautiful legs are a sin to cover with a dress.

Risqué Compliments

A compliment is a flower of language, so it should not be crude.

These compliments border on being risqué and should be used with great care and a good sense of humor. If you're not skilled at delivering them gracefully, it's better to avoid them.

−*What curves, and I'm without brakes!*

−*I wish I were a truck driver to navigate those curves.*

−*WOW, is that all yours, or is it rented?*

−*I'd love to be a French fry to go with that breast.*

−*Don't rock the cradle too much... you might wake the baby.*

−*Seeing you is something orgasmic.*

−*You're a walking Viagra.*

Astronomical Compliments

Since feminine beauty and femininity are full of mysteries, it's natural that they are compared to celestial bodies and stars.

−*With you, the night doesn't need stars.*

−*It's not the moon, but you who lights up the night.*

−*It's not the sun, but you who brightens the day.*

−*If the sun could see you... it would never be night.*

−*The sun has risen.*

−*A star is born.*

−*Your eyes have stolen the stars' shine from the sky.*

−*What is a star doing flying so low?*

–If every time I thought of you a star went out, there wouldn't be a single one left shining in the sky.

–If the moon ever calls your name... don't be surprised... I talk about you to her every night.

Botanical Compliments

Flowers, always associated with feminine beauty and delicacy, are frequent stars in many compliments.

–How can I give a flower to another flower?

–So many years as a gardener, and I've never seen a flower so beautiful.

–If all flowers were like you, I'd have a whole garden to myself.

–Who said flowers couldn't walk?

–What did science do to make flowers walk?

Pharmaceutical Compliments

Since feminine charms can ease any pain or soothe any anger, they have been associated with the effects of medicine.

–If beauty is medicine, you're the cure.

–You're like eye drops for my soul.

Police-Related Compliments

Sometimes, a gentleman is so impressed by a woman's charms that he compares their effects to a crime.

–If beauty were a crime, you'd be serving a life sentence.

–What you're doing should be illegal—it's a total theft!

–You're a heartbreaker!

–Man-slayer!

–You're ruthless!

–Your parents must have had trouble with the law because they stole all the blue from the sky and put it in your eyes.

"I Wish" Compliments

Many compliments begin with "I wish" as a declaration of the eternal desire to enjoy the magic of feminine charm.

–I wish I were a cat so I could spend my seven lives with you.

–I wish I were cross-eyed to see you twice.

–I wish I were a cup to pass by your lips and give you a kiss.

–I wish I were a movie camera to see you 24 times a second.

−I wish I were a tear to be born in your eyes, roll down your cheeks, and die on your lips.

−I wish I were a hummingbird to perch on that flower.

−I wish I were your favorite song so I could always be on your lips.

−I wish I were a pilot to fly through your dreams.

−I wish I were the best music to enter your ears and stir all your senses.

−I wish I were a sigh so my life could fade between your lips.

−I wish I were ice cream to melt in your mouth.

Religious Compliments

Feminine beauty can evoke such intense experiences that religious elements are often used to describe and praise it.

−When God created beauty, He was inspired by you.

−You were designed by an angel.

−What's going on up there that angels are walking on the sidewalk?

−Not even angels are as beautiful as you.

−You might not be the Virgin Mary, but you are full of grace.

−God made the world perfect, but He outdid Himself with you.

−The angels must be jealous because I now dream of you.

−What's happening in heaven that angels are falling to earth?

−The stars are mad at God because they weren't made as beautiful as you.

−Heaven must have granted permission for an angel like you to walk the earth.

−I'll give you a charm to ward off the evil eye.

Seismological Compliments

There's nothing like an earthquake to describe the impact of feminine charms.

−The earth trembles, mulata!

−Open up, earth, and swallow me!

−Every step you take is an earthquake.

Others

The list of elements to compare the positive effects of a lady on a gentleman is endless, making it difficult to classify all compliments. Here, I've grouped those that need others like them to form their own category.

−If only I were a pirate to steal that treasure.

−Why is the sky cloudy? Because all the blue is in your eyes.

−I wish you were the internet so I could surf your body.

−If beauty were a moment, you would be eternity.

−I don't need money or riches, your beauty is enough.

−You must have some flaw.

−You are a tribute to beauty.

−And they say monuments don't walk.

−Even your shadow dazzles.

−Is your dad a turner?

−Today, you're glowing!

−You look like a runway model.

−You look like you stepped out of a Michelangelo painting.

−Goodbye, bus!

−Goodbye, tank!

−The Andes mountain range is nothing compared to what you have.

−If you sweep like you walk, I'll become trash.

−You don't walk, you caress the ground with that beautiful stride.

−Let me get a scholarship to your heart.

−Look how well-distributed you are!

−Doll, which toy store did you escape from?

−Beautiful doll, step out of my dreams and into my life!

−There's so much to say to you, I'd rather stay silent.

−You're like a supermarket; you have it all!

−When your parents made you, they broke the mold.

−If only I were a cradle to rock that girl.

−Beautiful, you're a walking treasure.

*−I wrote your name on a wounded tree, and it's so beautiful that the tree
revived.*

−If I blink, I'll miss a moment of your beauty.

*−If I had to give you something, I'd give you a mirror, because the only
thing as beautiful as you is your reflection.*

−You're exaggerating, you can be pretty, but not that much.

−The only thing that surpasses your beauty is your intelligence.

−You're my favorite reason to lose sleep.

~~

WITTY SAYINGS AND DESCRIPTORS

A witty saying is a popular phrase that humorously expresses the sharpness of a people through the peculiarities of their language. The common folk coin these sayings and circulate them through everyday language. Some have a transitory nature, while others, due to their aptness in daily life, become established phrases. They resemble proverbs in their popular origin and simple yet clever construction; however, they don't become as proverbial since their structure doesn't allow it.

Unlike compliments, which are used to praise the positive qualities of women, the witty sayings collected here refer to both positive and negative qualities of both sexes but hold significant meaning within the context of courtship.

Persuasive and Flattering Man

Blessed are those with a sweet and timely way of speaking; great and pleasant is the power they possess.

−Sweet talker.

−Silver-tongued.

−He's got venom on the tip of his tongue.

−With his words, he can reach the stars.

−Makes gargles with flattery.

−If you let him talk, he could raise even his grandmother from the grave.

Well-Dressed Person

It's always worth emphasizing the importance of dressing well and presenting oneself nicely, without excess or deficiency, in any social interaction.

−They raided the wardrobe.

−Looks like a minister.

−Dressed like it's a wedding.

−More polished than a Sunday outfit.

−Looks like they stepped out of a magazine.

Indiscreet and Talkative Man

It seems some people enjoy talking about their "romantic conquests" more than the actual courtship or the subsequent union.

−King of the big mouth.

−Loudmouth.

−Neighborhood gossip.

−Two-legged gossip machine.

−Talks even about his mother.

−Has a tongue that trips him up.

−When he dies, he'll need two coffins—one for his body and another for his tongue.

Person Who Talks Nonstop and Doesn't Let Others Speak

Given that communication skills are crucial for effective courtship, not respecting turn-taking in conversation can be highly counterproductive.

−Chattering parrot.

−Crazy parrot.

−Cicada.

−Run away, or he'll make your ears bleed.

−Talks through their elbows.

−Mouth motor.

−Chattering bird.

Impertinent or Falsely Funny Person

Being unpleasant is so contrary to successful courtship that behaving this way is akin to anti-courtship. Nevertheless, there will always be a "nuisance" for a "nuisance."

−Annoying.

−Tedious.

−Pain in the neck.

−Unbearable.

−Insufferable.

−Pushy.

−Even his grandma can't stand him.

−Pain in the gut.

−Broken bridge.

−Lead pipe.

−Metal soup.

−Group ruiner.

−Dog's vomit.

−Worse than midnight colic.

−Hemorrhoidal thrombosis.

−No one can stomach him.

−When he arrives, it's time to leave.

−I can chew him, but I can't swallow him.

Woman Who Tends to Excite a Man Only to Later Reject Him

This behavior causes significant frustration for men.

−Flirt but won't commit.

−Turns up the heat but doesn't follow through.

−Lights the fire but doesn't put it out.

−String-along.

−All tease, no please.

−Bait and bail.

−Plays with fire but won't get burned.

−Gives the green light, then slams the brakes.

Lustful Man

These sayings capture the essence of those who relentlessly seek carnal pleasures in a disordered manner.

−Lives from the waist down.

−No crack he won't peek through.

−Doesn't even spare his grandmother.

−Can't see a skirt without chasing it.

−Always hunting for the next bed.

−His eyes undress every woman.

−A slave to his desires.

−Wherever there's temptation, he'll be there.

−Follows his instincts like a dog in heat.

~~

135

GLOSSARIES

In this section, the meaning of the most important terms used in this study is provided. They are organized alphabetically and according to the topic they belong to.

COURTSHIP

Affectionate Gestures: Acts of showing fondness or admiration, often through gifts, compliments, or kind deeds intended to win someone's favor.

Appearance: The external presentation of a person, including clothing, grooming, and personal hygiene, which plays a crucial role in first impressions during courtship.

Body Language: Non-verbal communication expressed through gestures, posture, facial expressions, and eye contact, revealing a person's true feelings and intentions.

Communication: The exchange of information, ideas, or emotions between two people. Effective communication in courtship involves both verbal and non-verbal cues to build connection.

Conquest: The successful act of winning someone's love or affection, often through persistent and skillful courtship efforts.

Coquetry: Playful, flirtatious behavior intended to attract or amuse someone, typically without serious intent.

Courtship: The process during which a couple develops a romantic relationship, often involving specific behaviors and rituals designed to attract a partner.

Curiosity: A strong desire to learn about someone, often driving interest and engagement during courtship.

Empathy: The ability to understand and share the feelings of another person, fostering deeper emotional connections in courtship.

Flattery: Compliments or praise directed at someone to win favor or affection, which must be sincere to be effective in courtship.

Persuasion: The act of convincing someone to believe or do something, particularly important in influencing emotions or decisions during courtship.

Rapport: A close and harmonious relationship where the individuals involved understand each other's feelings and communicate effectively, essential for successful courtship.

Romance: The expression of love and affection, often through special gestures, gifts, and actions that create excitement and mystery during courtship.

Seduction: The act of enticing someone into a romantic or sexual relationship, often through charm or manipulation.

Self-Control: The ability to manage one's emotions and impulses, crucial in courtship to avoid impulsive actions that could hinder the relationship.

Success in Courtship: Achieving the desired outcome in a romantic pursuit, typically marked by mutual affection and the beginning of a relationship.

Urbanity: Polite and refined behavior that reflects sophistication and good manners, important in making a positive impression during courtship.

Verbal Compliments: Words of praise directed at someone's appearance, personality, or actions, meant to convey admiration and attract their interest.

~~~

PARTNER SELECTION

Blunder: A significant mistake or error in judgment, often due to a lack of careful consideration.

Caution: The quality of being careful and avoiding unnecessary risks or dangers.

Defective Selection Criteria: Standards that are too lenient or poorly aligned with personal needs, leading to unproductive relationships.

Foolishness: The tendency to make unwise decisions, often lacking sound reasoning.

Foresight: The ability to anticipate future needs or challenges and prepare for them.

Good Judgment: The capacity to make well-reasoned and thoughtful decisions.

Impulsiveness: The tendency to act suddenly and without careful thought, often leading to rash decisions.

Inconsideration: A lack of thoughtfulness or concern for the feelings or circumstances of others.

Irrationality: Behaving in a way that lacks logic or sound reasoning.

Irresponsibility: Making decisions without considering the consequences or the need for careful planning.

Lightness: Treating important matters with insufficient seriousness or thought.

Maturity: The ability to handle life's challenges effectively and make wise decisions, reflecting emotional and mental development.
~~~

Precaution: The act of taking steps to prevent potential dangers or problems before they arise.

Premeditation: The process of planning or thinking through actions carefully before carrying them out.

Prudence: Exercising sound judgment and caution, especially in difficult situations.

Rationality: The quality of basing decisions and actions on logic and reason.

Recklessness: Acting with disregard for potential risks or consequences, often leading to negative outcomes.

Sagacity: The ability to make wise decisions based on foresight and insight.

Sanity: The state of having sound mental faculties, enabling rational decision-making.

Selection Criteria: Personal standards or guidelines used to determine acceptable or unacceptable partners, based on individual preferences and values.

Tact: The skill of handling delicate matters with care and consideration, avoiding offense and maintaining harmony.

Unattainable Selection Criteria: Unrealistically stringent standards that make it impossible to find a suitable partner.

Untimely Philosophizing: Engaging in deep thought or analysis at inappropriate times, leading to misguided actions.

~~~

DETECTION OF SEXUAL SIGNALS

Catathymia: Emotional distortion that alters perception, leading to a skewed view of reality. (See also **discernment** and **objectivity**)

Comprehension: The ability to understand the essence of things and problems.

Discernment: The ability to recognize and distinguish between different elements or situations.

Extracting Information: Skillfully obtaining information by encouraging someone to reveal what they know.

Indication: A sign or phenomenon suggesting the existence of something not directly observed.

Inquiry: The process of seeking information through questioning or investigation.
~~~

Insight: The ability to understand the true nature of a situation quickly and accurately.

Intelligence: The capacity to solve new situations and adapt effectively to circumstances.

Introspection: Examining one's own thoughts, feelings, and mental state.

Naivety: Innocence and a lack of malice or sophistication.

Objectivity: Adherence to reality and facts, viewing things as they truly are, rather than through personal bias.

Observation: The act of carefully examining or monitoring something.

Perceptiveness: The ability to notice and understand things quickly and accurately.

Prognosis: Predicting future outcomes based on current signs or indications.

Self-Deception: A psychological mechanism where an individual distorts reality to avoid confronting painful truths.

Sexual Signals: The various ways a woman consciously or unconsciously expresses her openness to being courted.

Sharpness: The ability to reason, understand complex situations quickly, and express ideas cleverly and wittily.

Stupidity: Foolishness or a notable lack of understanding or common sense.

Symptom: A sign or indication of something that is happening or is about to happen.

Symptomatology: The collection of signs or symptoms indicating a particular condition or situation.

Vivacity: The quality of being lively, energetic, and quick-witted.

Weak Points: The primary motives, goals, interests, and fears that influence a woman's life.

~~~

RELATIONSHIPS WITH OTHERS, ESPECIALLY WITH WOMEN

Acrimony: Harshness or bitterness in speech or behavior.

Affability: The quality of being pleasant and easy to talk to.

Aggressiveness: Overbearing or hostile behavior, often at the expense of others.

Assertiveness: The ability to stand up for oneself while respecting others.

Awkwardness: Clumsiness or a lack of grace in social situations.
~~~

Benevolence: Kindness and the desire to do good for others.

Bluntness: Directness that can be harsh or insensitive.

Boastfulness: Excessive pride in one's achievements, often expressed through bragging.

Caution: Careful consideration to avoid risks or dangers.

Chivalry: Courteous behavior, especially towards women.

Civility: Politeness and courtesy in behavior or speech.

Clinginess: Over-dependence on another person, often leading to feelings of suffocation.

Compliment: A polite expression of praise or admiration.

Criticism: The expression of disapproval based on perceived faults or mistakes.

Cunning: The ability to achieve goals through clever, often deceptive means.

Decorum: Proper behavior that shows respect and good manners.

Detachment: Emotional distance or lack of attachment.

Discretion: The quality of being careful in speech or actions to avoid offense or revealing private information.

Dullness: Lack of wit or liveliness in conversation.

Eloquence: The ability to speak or write fluently and persuasively.

False Modesty: Pretending to be modest while actually seeking attention or praise.

Flattery: Excessive or insincere praise intended to manipulate.

Garrulity: Excessive talkativeness, often without substance.

Generosity: Willingness to give freely, whether in terms of resources, time, or kindness.

Gracefulness: Elegance in movement and manner.

Humility: A modest view of one's importance.

Hypocrisy: The act of pretending to have beliefs, virtues, or feelings that one does not truly possess.

Impulsiveness: Acting without thought or consideration for the outcome.

Inarticulateness: Inability to express oneself clearly or effectively.

Indecorum: Lack of propriety or good taste in behavior.

Independence: Self-reliance and the ability to function without constant support.

Indifference: Lack of concern or interest in others.

Indifference: Lack of interest or concern, especially in social situations.

Indiscretion: Behavior or speech that reveals too much or shows a lack of good judgment.

Indiscretion: Lack of tactfulness, leading to inappropriate or offensive behavior.

Integrity: Adherence to moral and ethical principles, consistency in actions and words.

Meanness: Unkindness or spitefulness.

Misanthropy: Dislike or distrust of other people.

Modesty: The quality of being humble or moderate in one's self-assessment.

Modesty: The quality of being unassuming about one's abilities.

Naivety: Lack of experience or sophistication, often leading to vulnerability.

Passivity: The acceptance of events without active response or resistance.

Recklessness: Disregard for the consequences of one's actions.

Rudeness: The quality of being impolite or disrespectful.

Selfishness: Concern only for oneself, often at the expense of others.

Silliness: Foolishness or a lack of seriousness, often inappropriately so.

Sincerity: Genuineness in feelings, beliefs, and actions.

Sincerity: Honesty and straightforwardness in actions and speech.

Sociability: The tendency to seek and enjoy social interactions.

Social Ease: The ability to interact smoothly and comfortably with others.

Stinginess: Reluctance to give or share.

Tact: The ability to handle difficult situations delicately without causing offense.

Tactlessness: Lack of sensitivity in dealing with others, often leading to offense.

Unsociability: Reluctance or inability to engage socially.

Vanity: Excessive pride in one's appearance or achievements.

Vulgarity: Coarse or unrefined behavior or speech.

Witticism: A clever and humorous remark.

~~~

SELF-CONTROL
~~~

Abstinence: Refraining from satisfying desires or appetites, either partially or completely, when necessary.

Acceptance: The ability to endure adversities that cannot be changed.

Agitation: Emotional instability leading to loss of calmness.

Audacity: Boldness and courage in taking decisive actions.

Boldness: The willingness to take risks and make daring moves.

Brashness: Reckless boldness without regard for consequences.

Conformity: Acceptance of situations that could and should be improved but are not.

Courage: The resolute effort to face challenges and adversity.

Cowardice: Lack of courage to confront challenges or difficulties.

Despair: Loss of hope or belief in positive outcomes and surrender to adverse situations.

Detachment: Withdrawal from emotional involvement, often to an unhealthy extent.

Determination: The firm resolve to achieve a goal.

Diligence: The prompt and energetic execution of tasks or duties.

Emotional Instability: Frequent and extreme emotional fluctuations.

Emotional Suppression: The intentional avoidance of expressing emotions, leading to potential psychological strain.

Equanimity: The ability to remain calm and composed in both success and failure.

Flexibility: The ability to adapt to changing circumstances or needs.

Foolhardiness: Rashness and disregard for potential dangers.

Giving Up: Abandoning efforts when faced with difficulties.

Hesitation: Uncertainty in taking actions or making decisions.

Hope: A state of mind that perceives desired outcomes as possible.

Impatience: The inability to tolerate delays or endure challenges calmly.

Impulsiveness: Acting on immediate desires without considering long-term consequences.

Inconstancy: Lack of steadiness or persistence in pursuing goals.

Indecisiveness: Difficulty in making decisions and acting on them.

Indulgence: Excessive yielding to desires or impulses.

Inflexibility: Stubborn adherence to a particular course of action or thought, regardless of circumstances.

Lack of Self-Control: Inability to manage one's impulses, leading to inappropriate actions.

Laziness: The habit of avoiding effort or responsibility.

Lethargy: A state of sluggishness or lack of enthusiasm.

Obstinacy: Unwillingness to change one's course of action or opinion despite reasonable arguments or evidence.

Overindulgence: Excessive and unrestrained fulfillment of desires.

Passivity: Failing to take action when needed, resulting in missed opportunities.

Patience: The capacity to endure discomfort, delays, or challenges without losing composure.

Perseverance: The determination to continue pursuing a goal despite obstacles.

Pessimism: The tendency to expect the worst in all situations.

Procrastination: The act of delaying tasks or decisions unnecessarily.

Recklessness: Taking bold actions without considering the consequences.

Resignation: Accepting negative situations without attempting to improve them.

Resignation: Accepting unfavorable circumstances without attempting to change them.

Restlessness: A constant need for activity or change due to an inability to remain calm.

Rigidity: Inability to adjust or change in response to new information or situations.

Self-Control: The ability to regulate impulses, desires, and emotions in line with long-term goals.

Stoicism: The ability to endure pain or hardship without showing emotions.

Stubbornness: Refusing to change one's mind or course of action even when it is counterproductive.

Tenacity: The persistent pursuit of a goal despite challenges.

Timidity: Shyness or a lack of bravery in facing difficult situations.

Vigor: The energy and strength required to carry out tasks effectively.

Weakness: Lack of strength or energy, both physically and morally.

~~~

BIBLIOGRAPHIC REFERENCES AND NOTES

1- Even if you don't have difficulties in this area, a text like this, which collects the experiences of many, could improve your performance in courtship.

2- Sánchez Hernández Arturo José. The Impact of Ethical-Moral, Artistic-Aesthetic, and Scientific-Technological Values on the Excellence of Psychiatry Services. Rev. Hum. Med. [online journal]. 2007 Apr [cited 2012 May 21]; 7(1):. Available at: http://scielo.sld.cu/scielo.php?script=sci_arttext&pid=S1727-81202007000100005&lng=es.

3- Vishnu Sarma. Panchatantra. Havana. Cuba. Editorial Arte y Literatura; 1989.

4- Vatsyayana. Kamasutra. Erotic Literature. Libros en Red; 2000.

5- Ovid. The Art of Love. Remedies for Love. Cosmetics for the Female Face. Madrid. Spain. Ediciones AKAL; 1991.

6- Fromm, Erich. The Art of Loving. Barcelona. Spain. Ediciones Paidós; 2007.

7- Masters WH, Johnson VE, Kolodny RC. Human Sexuality. Havana. Cuba. Editorial Científico Técnica; 1987. Pp. 349-377.

8- Hilgert Alex. Bible of Seduction. Brazil. Editora PONTHANIUM; 1995.

9- Luna Mario. Sex Code. The Practical Manual of Seduction Masters. Madrid. Spain. Ediciones Nowtilus; 2007.

10- Andrade Arturo. Secrets of Seduction for Men. How to Master the Art of Seduction Safely and Naturally. School of Seduction; 2007. Available at URL: http://www.escueladeseduccion.org.

11- Nicholas Margaret. The World's Greatest Lovers. Mexico. Editorial Diana; 1990.

12- Ravelo Aloyma. Sex, Love, and Eroticism. Words that Provoke. Havana. Cuba. Editorial de la Mujer; 2011. Pp. 97-131.

13- With aphorisms, sayings, maxims, and proverbs, one gains privileged access to the non-dominant hemisphere of the brain, which is closer to experiences, emotions, and the essential synthesis than the dominant hemisphere. (Clavijo Portieles Alberto. Crisis, Family, and Psychotherapy. Second Edition. Havana. Cuba. Editorial Ciencias Médicas; 2011. p. 176.

14- The qualities in this second group are nuances of prudence, but they have been treated separately because they are related to different aspects of courtship.

15- Aristotle. *Nicomachean Ethics * Politics. Mexico. Editorial Porrúa, S.A.; 1992. p. 18-27, 23, 26.*

16- Sintes Pros Jorge. *Dictionary of Aphorisms, Sayings, and Sayings. Barcelona. Spain. Editorial Sintes; 1954. p. 290.*

17- Martí José. *Notions of Logic. On Fallacies. In: Complete Works, Vol. XXV. Havana. Cuba. Editorial de Ciencias Sociales; 1991. p. 338.*

18- Martí José. *Notions of Logic. On Fallacies. In: Complete Works, Vol. XXV. Havana. Cuba. Editorial de Ciencias Sociales; 1991. p. 338.*

19- Vatsyayana *(between the 1st and 6th centuries CE) was an Indian religious scholar and writer during the Gupta Empire. His most important work was the Kama Sutra, which deals with human sexual behavior and dedicates two entire chapters to the art of sexually attracting another person. See: Vatsyayana. Kamasutra. Erotic Literature. Libros en Red; 2000.*

20- Publius Ovidius Naso *(43 BCE - c. 17 CE), Roman poet of great popularity from his time to the present. Among his notable works are: "The Art of Love" and "Remedies for Love." The former covers topics such as: where to find women, how to court and conquer them, how to maintain love, regain it, or prevent it from being stolen. The latter offers advice and strategies to avoid the harm that love can cause. See: Ovid. The Art of Love. Remedies for Love. Cosmetics for the Female Face. Madrid. Spain. Ediciones AKAL; 1991.*

21- Erich Fromm *(1900-1980) was a prominent psychoanalyst, social psychologist, and humanist philosopher of Jewish-German origin. In his work also titled The Art of Loving, he posits that love can be the product of theoretical study because it is an art, and mastering any art requires deep understanding of both theory and practice. See: Fromm Erich. The Art of Loving. Barcelona. Spain. Ediciones Paidós; 2007.*

22- *Women were asked: How would you like to be courted? What qualities would you like the man who courts you to have? What qualities would you reject in a man who is courting you? How do women behave when they want a partner or are interested in a man? The questions asked to the men were: How do you think effective courtship is done? What qualities do you think are necessary for effective courtship? What qualities hinder effective courtship? How do women behave when they need a partner or are interested in a man?*

23- Clavijo Portieles Alberto. *Crisis, Family, and Psychotherapy. Second Edition. Havana. Cuba. Editorial Ciencias Médicas; 2011. pp. 183-187.*

24- Feijóo Samuel. *The Knowledge of Juan Without Anything. Signs in the Expression of the People. Saying.* Santa Clara. Cuba. Revista Signos. No 14. Year 5, No 2; January-April 1974. p.14.

25- Carnegie Dale. *How to Win Friends and Influence People.* Rosario. Argentina. Biblioteca del Nuevo Tiempo. 104th edition: September 1996. p. 40. Affiliated with: Directorio Promineo: *www.promineo.gq.nu*.

26- Feijóo Samuel. *The Knowledge of Juan Without Anything. Signs in the Expression of the People. Saying.* Santa Clara. Cuba. Revista Signos. No 14. Year 5, No 2; January-April 1974. p. 128.

27- Feijóo Samuel. *The Knowledge of Juan Without Anything. Signs in the Expression of the People. Saying.* Santa Clara. Cuba. Revista Signos. No 14. Year 5, No 2; January-April 1974. p. 110.

28- Maldonado Felipe CR. *Being and Time. Themes of Spain. Classic Spanish Refranes and Other Popular Sayings.* Madrid. Spain. Taurus Ediciones S.A.; 1960. p. 75.

29- Solís José Antonio. *Sayings, Proverbs, and Maxims. The Whole Treasure of Popular Wisdom.* Spain. El Arca de Papel Editores; 2003. p.27.

30- Solís José Antonio. *Sayings, Proverbs, and Maxims. The Whole Treasure of Popular Wisdom of the Peoples of Spain Within Your Reach.* Spain. El Arca de Papel Editores; 2003. p.153.

31- Feijóo Samuel. *The Knowledge of Juan Without Anything. Signs in the Expression of the People. Saying.* Santa Clara. Cuba. Revista Signos. No 14. Year 5, No 2; January-April 1974. p. 54.

32- Self-confidence and its possible deviations are discussed in Chapter Four.

33- Solís José Antonio. *Sayings, Proverbs, and Maxims. The Whole Treasure of Popular Wisdom of the Peoples of Spain Within Your Reach.* Spain. El Arca de Papel Editores; 2003. p.29.

34- Sintes Pros Jorge. *Dictionary of Aphorisms, Proverbs, and Sayings.* Barcelona. Spain. Editorial Sintes; 1954. p. 183.

35- Feijóo Samuel. *The Knowledge of Juan Without Anything. Signs in the Expression of the People. Saying.* Santa Clara. Cuba. Revista Signos. No 14. Year 5, No 2; January-April 1974. p. 200.

36- Solís José Antonio. *Sayings, Proverbs, and Maxims. The Whole Treasure of Popular Wisdom of the Peoples of Spain Within Your Reach.* Spain. El Arca de Papel Editores; 2003. p.123.

37- Solarte Mejia Lidardo. *Sayings and Maxims.* Bogotá. Colombia. Editora Dosmil; 1979. p. 16.

38- Valdés Jane Ernesto. Divinatory Sayings of the Caracol and the Odun of Ifá. -In Cuban Santería- Documents for the History and Culture of Osha-Ifá in Cuba. Sayings from (6-3) Obara tonti Ogundá, from (10-4) Ofún tonti Iroso, from Ofun Koso and from Ogunda Ka. First Edition: Proyecto Orunmila; 2007. p. 21, 41, 102, 125.

39- Feijóo Samuel. From Compliments to Witty Remarks, Oral Folklore of Cuba. Havana. Cuba. Editorial Letras Cubanas; 1981. p. 55.

40- Feijóo Samuel. The Knowledge of Juan Without Anything. Signs in the Expression of the People. Saying. Santa Clara. Cuba. Revista Signos. No 14. Year 5, No 2; January-April 1974. p. 124.

41- Rovira Àlex. Words That Heal. Barcelona. Spain. Plataforma Editorial. 2008. p.25.

42- Solís José Antonio. Sayings, Proverbs, and Maxims. The Whole Treasure of Popular Wisdom of the Peoples of Spain Within Your Reach. Spain. El Arca de Papel Editores; 2003. p.79.

43- Often, the tendency to boast comes from deep insecurities and conflicts, which the individual tries to deny both to others and to themselves through these exaggerations, which, if true, would negate the existence of their problems. Popular wisdom summarizes this well in the saying: "Tell me what you boast about, and I'll tell you what you lack." (Clavijo Portieles Alberto. Crisis, Family, and Psychotherapy. Second Edition. Havana. Cuba. Editorial Ciencias Médicas; 2011. p.35.

44- Solís José Antonio. Sayings, Proverbs, and Maxims. The Whole Treasure of Popular Wisdom of the Peoples of Spain Within Your Reach. Spain. El Arca de Papel Editores; 2003. p.79.

45- The saying collected by José Antonio Solís is: "What one denies, another begs for." In: Solís José Antonio. Sayings, Proverbs, and Maxims. The Whole Treasure of Popular Wisdom of the Peoples of Spain Within Your Reach. Spain. El Arca de Papel Editores; 2003. p.93.

46- Feijóo Samuel. The Knowledge of Juan Without Anything. Signs in the Expression of the People. Saying. Santa Clara. Cuba. Revista Signos. No 14. Year 5, No 2; January-April 1974. p.56.

47- Martí José. Our America. Theater. The Iron Chain. Drama by Agustín Cuenca. In: Complete Works, Vol. VI. Havana. Cuba. Editorial de Ciencias Sociales; 1991. p. 453.

48- Valdés Jane Ernesto. Divinatory Sayings of the Caracol and the Odun of Ifá. -In Cuban Santería- Documents for the History and Culture of Osha-Ifá in Cuba. Sayings from (10-1) Ofún tonti Okana. First Edition: Proyecto Orunmila; 2007. p. 40.

49- Cicero in Sintes Pros Jorge. Great Dictionary of Famous Phrases. Barcelona. Spain. Editorial Sintes; 1960. p. 151.

50- Feijóo Samuel. The Knowledge of Juan Without Anything. Signs in the Expression of the People. Saying. Santa Clara. Cuba. Revista Signos. No 14. Year 5, No 2; January-April 1974. p. 137.

51- Solís José Antonio. Sayings, Proverbs, and Maxims. The Whole Treasure of Popular Wisdom of the Peoples of Spain Within Your Reach. Spain. El Arca de Papel Editores; 2003. p.109.

52- Feijóo Samuel. The Knowledge of Juan Without Anything. Signs in the Expression of the People. Saying. Santa Clara. Cuba. Revista Signos. No 14. Year 5, No 2; January-April 1974. p. 53.

53- The original saying compiled by Samuel Feijóo is: "One takes the form of the stick they lean on." Feijóo Samuel. The Knowledge of Juan Without Anything. Signs in the Expression of the People. Saying. Santa Clara. Cuba. Revista Signos. No 14. Year 5, No 2; January-April 1974. p.88.

54- Feijóo Samuel. The Knowledge of Juan Without Anything. Signs in the Expression of the People. Saying. Santa Clara. Cuba. Revista Signos. No 14. Year 5, No 2; January-April 1974. p. 55.

55- Feijóo Samuel. The Knowledge of Juan Without Anything. Signs in the Expression of the People. Saying. Santa Clara. Cuba. Revista Signos. No 14. Year 5, No 2; January-April 1974. p. 93.

56- Solís José Antonio. Sayings, Proverbs, and Maxims. The Whole Treasure of Popular Wisdom of the Peoples of Spain Within Your Reach. Spain. El Arca de Papel Editores; 2003. p.86.

57- Solís José Antonio. Sayings, Proverbs, and Maxims. The Whole Treasure of Popular Wisdom of the Peoples of Spain Within Your Reach. Spain. El Arca de Papel Editores; 2003. p. 84.

58- The saying collected by Samuel Flores-Huerta is: "With the saints, you will be a saint; with the lost, you will be lost." In: Flores-Huerta Samuel. Sayings or Proverbs. Thematic Compendium. Mexico. CopIt-arXives; 2016. p.64. Available at URL:

59- Martí José. Complete Works. Vol II. Commemorative edition of the fiftieth anniversary of his death. Havana. Cuba. Editorial Lex; 1946. p. 1668.

60- The saying collected by Jorge Sintes Pros is: "A good woman makes a full house out of an empty one." In: Sintes Pros Jorge. Dictionary of Aphorisms, Sayings, and Sayings. Barcelona. Spain. Editorial Sintes; 1954. p. 192.

61- Both the female and male roles are important in raising children. When both types of functions are adequately fulfilled, it is said that we are in the presence of positive mothering and fathering. (Clavijo Portieles Alberto. Crisis, Family, and Psychotherapy. Second Edition. Havana. Cuba. Editorial Ciencias Médicas; 2011. p. 107.

62- The saying collected by José Antonio Solís is: "The worth of a woman is seen in her children." In: Solís José Antonio. Sayings, Proverbs, and Maxims. The Whole Treasure of Popular Wisdom. Spain. El Arca de Papel Editores; 2003. p.93.

63- Dios Habla Hoy. The Bible with Deuterocanonicals. Popular Version. Second Edition. Mexico City. United Bible Societies; 1987. p.115.

64- Dios Habla Hoy. The Bible with Deuterocanonicals. Popular Version. Second Edition. Mexico City. United Bible Societies; 1987. p.598.

65- Dios Habla Hoy. The Bible with Deuterocanonicals. Popular Version. Second Edition. Mexico City. United Bible Societies; 1987. p.598.

66- Dios Habla Hoy. The Bible with Deuterocanonicals. Popular Version. Second Edition. Mexico City. United Bible Societies; 1987. p.605.

67- Solís José Antonio. Sayings, Proverbs, and Maxims. Spain. El Arca de Papel Editores; 2003. p. 107.

68- Feijóo Samuel. The Knowledge of Juan Without Anything. Signs in the Expression of the People. Saying. Santa Clara. Cuba. Revista Signos. No 14. Year 5, No 2; January-April 1974. p. 104.

69- Sintes Pros Jorge. Dictionary of Aphorisms, Sayings, and Sayings. Barcelona. Spain. Editorial Sintes; 1954. p. 152.

70- Solís José Antonio. Sayings, Proverbs, and Maxims. The Whole Treasure of Popular Wisdom. Spain. El Arca de Papel Editores; 2003. p.42.

71) Álvarez de los Ríos Tomás. The Book of Sayings. Camagüey. Cuba: Editorial Ácana; 2017. p. 43.

72- Feijóo Samuel. The Knowledge of Juan Without Anything. Signs in the Expression of the People. Saying. Santa Clara. Cuba. Revista Signos. No 14. Year 5, No 2; January-April 1974. p. 52.

73- The saying collected by José Antonio Solís is: "Don't look for in the plaza what you have at home." In: Solís José Antonio. Sayings, Proverbs, and Maxims. The Whole Treasure of Popular Wisdom of the Peoples of Spain Within Your Reach. Spain. El Arca de Papel Editores; 2003. p. 111.

74- Solís José Antonio. Sayings, Proverbs, and Maxims. The Whole Treasure of Popular Wisdom of the Peoples of Spain Within Your Reach. Spain. El Arca de Papel Editores; 2003. p. 106.

75- Valdés Jane Ernesto. *Divinatory Sayings of the Caracol and the Odun of Ifá. -In Cuban Santería- Documents for the History and Culture of Osha-Ifá in Cuba. Sayings from (3-6) Ogundá tonti Obara.* First Edition: Proyecto Orunmila; 2007. p. 10.

76- Solís José Antonio. *Sayings, Proverbs, and Maxims. The Whole Treasure of Popular Wisdom of the Peoples of Spain Within Your Reach.* Spain. El Arca de Papel Editores; 2003. p.86.

77- Solís José Antonio. *Sayings, Proverbs, and Maxims. The Whole Treasure of Popular Wisdom of the Peoples of Spain Within Your Reach.* Spain. El Arca de Papel Editores; 2003. p. 86.

78- The saying collected by José Antonio Solís is: "You will seek the good and avoid the bad." In: Solís José Antonio. *Sayings, Proverbs, and Maxims. The Whole Treasure of Popular Wisdom of the Peoples of Spain Within Your Reach.* Spain. El Arca de Papel Editores; 2003. p.19.

79- The qualities promoted for a "good woman" differ from one culture to another.

80- Feijóo Samuel. *The Knowledge of Juan Without Anything. Signs in the Expression of the People. Saying.* Santa Clara. Cuba. Revista Signos. No 14. Year 5, No 2; January-April 1974. p. 54.

81- Solís José Antonio. *Sayings, Proverbs, and Maxims. The Whole Treasure of Popular Wisdom of the Peoples of Spain Within Your Reach.* Spain. El Arca de Papel Editores; 2003. p.93.

82- The saying collected by José Antonio Solís is: "What one denies, another begs for." In: Solís José Antonio. *Sayings, Proverbs, and Maxims. The Whole Treasure of Popular Wisdom of the Peoples of Spain Within Your Reach.* Spain. El Arca de Papel Editores; 2003. p.93.

83- Feijóo Samuel. *The Knowledge of Juan Without Anything. Signs in the Expression of the People. Saying.* Santa Clara. Cuba. Revista Signos. No 14. Year 5, No 2; January-April 1974. p. 183.

84- Feijóo Samuel. *The Knowledge of Juan Without Anything. Signs in the Expression of the People. Saying.* Santa Clara. Cuba. Revista Signos. No 14. Year 5, No 2; January-April 1974. p. 178.

85- Feijóo Samuel. *The Knowledge of Juan Without Anything. Signs in the Expression of the People. Saying.* Santa Clara. Cuba. Revista Signos. No 14. Year 5, No 2; January-April 1974. p.208.

86- Feijóo Samuel. *From Compliments to Witty Remarks, Oral Folklore of Cuba.* Havana. Cuba. Editorial Letras Cubanas; 1981. p. 37.

87- *Feijóo Samuel. From Compliments to Witty Remarks, Oral Folklore of Cuba. Havana. Cuba. Editorial Letras Cubanas; 1981. p. 26.*

88- *Feijóo Samuel. The Knowledge of Juan Without Anything. Signs in the Expression of the People. Saying. Santa Clara. Cuba. Revista Signos. No 14. Year 5, No 2; January-April 1974. p. 178.*

89- *Feijóo Samuel. From Compliments to Witty Remarks, Oral Folklore of Cuba. Havana. Cuba. Editorial Letras Cubanas; 1981. p. 24.*

90- *Sintes Pros Jorge. Dictionary of Aphorisms, Sayings, and Sayings. Barcelona. Spain. Editorial Sintes; 1954. p. 216.*

91- *Feijóo Samuel. The Knowledge of Juan Without Anything. Signs in the Expression of the People. Saying. Santa Clara. Cuba. Revista Signos. No 14. Year 5, No 2; January-April 1974. p. 99.*

92- *Feijóo Samuel. From Compliments to Witty Remarks, Oral Folklore of Cuba. Havana. Cuba. Editorial Letras Cubanas; 1981. p. 54.*

93- *Feijóo Samuel. The Knowledge of Juan Without Anything. Signs in the Expression of the People. Saying. Santa Clara. Cuba. Revista Signos. No 14. Year 5, No 2; January-April 1974. p. 110.*

94- *Feijóo Samuel. The Knowledge of Juan Without Anything. Signs in the Expression of the People. Saying. Santa Clara. Cuba. Revista Signos. No 14. Year 5, No 2; January-April 1974. p. 100.*

95- *Álvarez de los Ríos Tomás. The Book of Suyings. Camagüey. Cuba: Editorial Ácana; 2017. p. 52.*

96- *Feijóo Samuel. From Compliments to Witty Remarks, Oral Folklore of Cuba. Havana. Cuba. Editorial Letras Cubanas; 1981. p. 46.*

97- *Feijóo Samuel. The Knowledge of Juan Without Anything. Signs in the Expression of the People. Saying. Santa Clara. Cuba. Revista Signos. No 14. Year 5, No 2; January-April 1974. p. 99.*

98- *Feijóo Samuel. The Knowledge of Juan Without Anything. Signs in the Expression of the People. Saying. Santa Clara. Cuba. Revista Signos. No 14. Year 5, No 2; January-April 1974. p. 206.*

99- *Solís José Antonio. Sayings, Proverbs, and Maxims. The Whole Treasure of Popular Wisdom. Spain. El Arca de Papel Editores; 2003. p.42.*

100- *Cannobbio Agustín. Chilean Sayings. Santiago de Chile. Chile: Encuadernación Barcelona; 1901. p. 37.*

101- *Feijóo Samuel. The Knowledge of Juan Without Anything. Signs in the Expression of the People. Saying. Santa Clara. Cuba. Revista Signos. No 14. Year 5, No 2; January-April 1974. p. 126.*

102- Feijóo Samuel. *The Knowledge of Juan Without Anything. Signs in the Expression of the People. Saying. Santa Clara. Cuba. Revista Signos. No 14. Year 5, No 2; January-April 1974. p. 89.*

103- Solís José Antonio. *Sayings, Proverbs, and Maxims. The Whole Treasure of Popular Wisdom of the Peoples of Spain Within Your Reach. Spain. El Arca de Papel Editores; 2003. p.127.*

104- Solís José Antonio. *Sayings, Proverbs, and Maxims. The Whole Treasure of Popular Wisdom of the Peoples of Spain Within Your Reach. Spain. El Arca de Papel Editores; 2003. p.127.*

105- Álvarez de los Ríos Tomás. *The Book of Sayings. Camagüey. Cuba: Editorial Ácana; 2017. p. 95.*

106- Flores-Huerta Samuel. *Sayings or Proverbs. Thematic Compendium. Mexico: CopIt-arXives; 2016. p. 146.*

107- Feijóo Samuel. *The Knowledge of Juan Without Anything. Signs in the Expression of the People. Saying. Santa Clara. Cuba. Revista Signos. No 14. Year 5, No 2; January-April 1974. p.15.*

108- Feijóo Samuel. *The Knowledge of Juan Without Anything. Signs in the Expression of the People. Saying. Santa Clara. Cuba. Revista Signos. No 14. Year 5, No 2; January-April 1974. p. 113.*

109- Dale Carnegie repeatedly emphasizes in his work: *How to Win Friends and Influence People,* the importance of the ability to see things from others' perspectives in order to achieve success. (Carnegie Dale. *How to Win Friends and Influence People. Rosario. Argentina. Biblioteca del Nuevo Tiempo. 104th edition; 1996. pp. 8, 21, 22, 23, 24, 25, 48, 61, 65, 66, 67.)*

110- Feijóo Samuel. *The Knowledge of Juan Without Anything. Signs in the Expression of the People. Saying. Santa Clara. Cuba. Revista Signos. No 14. Year 5, No 2; January-April 1974. p. 86.*

111- Feijóo Samuel. *The Knowledge of Juan Without Anything. Signs in the Expression of the People. Saying. Santa Clara. Cuba. Revista Signos. No 14. Year 5, No 2; January-April 1974. p. 52.*

112- Feijóo Samuel. *The Knowledge of Juan Without Anything. Signs in the Expression of the People. Saying. Santa Clara. Cuba. Revista Signos. No 14. Year 5, No 2; January-April 1974. p. 135.*

113- Sintes Pros Jorge. *Dictionary of Aphorisms, Sayings, and Sayings. Barcelona. Spain. Editorial Sintes; 1954. p.167.*

114- Solís José Antonio. *Sayings, Proverbs, and Maxims. The Whole Treasure of Popular Wisdom of the Peoples of Spain Within Your Reach. Spain. El Arca de Papel Editores; 2003. p.20.*

115- *Clavijo Portieles Alberto. Crisis, Family, and Psychotherapy. Second Edition. Havana. Cuba. Editorial Ciencias Médicas; 2011. p.30.*

116- *Feijóo Samuel. The Knowledge of Juan Without Anything. Signs in the Expression of the People. Saying. Santa Clara. Cuba. Revista Signos. No 14. Year 5, No 2; January-April 1974. p. 51.*

117- *Feijóo Samuel. The Knowledge of Juan Without Anything. Signs in the Expression of the People. Saying. Santa Clara. Cuba. Revista Signos. No 14. Year 5, No 2; January-April 1974. p. 203.*

118- *Flores-Huerta Samuel. Sayings or Proverbs. Thematic Compendium. Mexico. CopIt-arXives; 2016. p. 45. Available at URL:*

119- *Feijóo Samuel. The Knowledge of Juan Without Anything. Signs in the Expression of the People. Saying. Santa Clara. Cuba. Revista Signos. No 14. Year 5, No 2; January-April 1974. p. 54.*

120- *Flores-Huerta Samuel. Sayings or Proverbs. Thematic Compendium. Mexico. CopIt-arXives; 2016. p. 46. Available at URL:*

121- *Feijóo Samuel. The Knowledge of Juan Without Anything. Signs in the Expression of the People. Saying. Santa Clara. Cuba. Revista Signos. No 14. Year 5, No 2; January-April 1974. p. 52.*

122- *Valdés Jane Ernesto. Divinatory Sayings of the Caracol and the Odun of Ifá. -In Cuban Santería- Documents for the History and Culture of Osha-Ifá in Cuba. First Edition: Proyecto Orunmila; 2007. p. 20. Available at URL:*

123- *Vishnu Sarma. Panchatantra. Havana. Cuba. Editorial Arte y Literatura; 1989, p. 374.*

124- *Maldonado Felipe CR. Being and Time. Themes of Spain. Classic Spanish Sayings and Other Popular Sayings. Madrid. Spain. Taurus Ediciones S.A.; 1960. p. 53.*

125- *Feijóo Samuel. The Knowledge of Juan Without Anything. Signs in the Expression of the People. Saying. Santa Clara. Cuba. Revista Signos. No 14. Year 5, No 2; January-April 1974. p. 63.*

126- *Solarte Mejia Lidardo. Sayings and Maxims. Bogotá. Colombia. Editora Dosmil; 1979. p. 101.*

127- *Feijóo Samuel. The Knowledge of Juan Without Anything. Signs in the Expression of the People. Saying. Santa Clara. Cuba. Revista Signos. No 14. Year 5, No 2; January-April 1974. p. 199.*

128- *Solís José Antonio. Sayings, Proverbs, and Maxims. The Whole Treasure of Popular Wisdom. Spain. El Arca de Papel Editores; 2003. p. 68.*

129- Clavijo Portieles Alberto. *Crisis, Family, and Psychotherapy*. Second Edition. Havana. Cuba. Editorial Ciencias Médicas; 2011. p.31.

130- Maldonado Felipe CR. *Being and Time. Themes of Spain. Classic Spanish Sayings and Other Popular Sayings*. Madrid. Spain. Taurus Ediciones S.A.; 1960. p. 124.

131- Valdés Jane Ernesto. *Divinatory Sayings of the Caracol and the Odun of Ifá. -In Cuban Santería- Documents for the History and Culture of Osha-Ifá in Cuba. Sayings from (14-3) Merinlá tonti Ogundá*. First Edition: Proyecto Orunmila; 2007. p. 57. Available at:

132- Valdés Jane Ernesto. *Divinatory Sayings of the Caracol and the Odun of Ifá. -In Cuban Santería- Documents for the History and Culture of Osha-Ifá in Cuba. Sayings from (12-13) Eyilá tonti Metanlá*. First Edition: Proyecto Orunmila; 2007. p. 53. Available at :

133- Feijóo Samuel. *The Knowledge of Juan Without Anything. Signs in the Expression of the People. Saying*. Santa Clara. Cuba. Revista Signos. No 14. Year 5, No 2; January-April 1974. p. 142.

134- Solís José Antonio. *Sayings, Proverbs, and Maxims. The Whole Treasure of Popular Wisdom of the Peoples of Spain Within Your Reach*. Spain. El Arca de Papel Editores; 2003. p.131.

135- Feijóo Samuel. *The Knowledge of Juan Without Anything. Signs in the Expression of the People. Saying*. Santa Clara. Cuba. Revista Signos. No 14. Year 5, No 2; January-April 1974. p. 143.

136- Solís José Antonio. *Sayings, Proverbs, and Maxims. The Whole Treasure of Popular Wisdom of the Peoples of Spain Within Your Reach*. Spain. El Arca de Papel Editores; 2003. p.36.

137- Solís José Antonio. *Sayings, Proverbs, and Maxims. The Whole Treasure of Popular Wisdom of the Peoples of Spain Within Your Reach*. Spain. El Arca de Papel Editores; 2003. p.27.

138- Carnegie Dale. *How to Win Friends and Influence People*. Rosario. Argentina. Biblioteca del Nuevo Tiempo. 104th edition: September 1996. p. 10. Affiliated with: Directorio Promineo: *www.promineo.gq.nu*.

139- Solís José Antonio. *Sayings, Proverbs, and Maxims. The Whole Treasure of Popular Wisdom of the Peoples of Spain Within Your Reach*. Spain. El Arca de Papel Editores; 2003. p.126.

140- Feijóo Samuel. *The Knowledge of Juan Without Anything. Signs in the Expression of the People. Saying*. Santa Clara. Cuba. Revista Signos. No 14. Year 5, No 2; January-April 1974. p. 81.

141- Feijóo Samuel. The Knowledge of Juan Without Anything. Signs in the Expression of the People. Saying. Santa Clara. Cuba. Revista Signos. No 14. Year 5, No 2; January-April 1974. p. 68.

142- Feijóo Samuel. The Knowledge of Juan Without Anything. Signs in the Expression of the People. Saying. Santa Clara. Cuba. Revista Signos. No 14. Year 5, No 2; January-April 1974. p. 151.

143- Feijóo Samuel. From Compliments to Witty Remarks, Oral Folklore of Cuba. Havana. Cuba. Editorial Letras Cubanas; 1981. p. 44.

144- The saying compiled by Samuel Feijóo is: "Goodness is often mistaken for foolishness," but goodness, in its time and measure, holds great value and should not be mistaken for foolishness, which is more aligned with spinelessness. (Feijóo Samuel. The Knowledge of Juan Without Anything. Signs in the Expression of the People. Saying. Santa Clara. Cuba. Revista Signos. No 14. Year 5, No 2; January-April 1974. p. 104).

145- Feijóo Samuel. The Knowledge of Juan Without Anything. Signs in the Expression of the People. Saying. Santa Clara. Cuba. Revista Signos. No 14. Year 5, No 2; January-April 1974. p. 186.

146- Dios Habla Hoy. The Bible with Deuterocanonical Books. Popular Version. Second Edition. Mexico D.F. United Bible Societies; 1987. p. 612.

147- Feijóo Samuel. The Knowledge of Juan Without Anything. Signs in the Expression of the People. Saying. Santa Clara. Cuba. Revista Signos. No 14. Year 5, No 2; January-April 1974. p. 114.

148- Carnegie Dale. How to Win Friends and Influence People. Rosario. Argentina. Biblioteca del Nuevo Tiempo. 104th edition: September 1996. p. 61. Affiliated with: Directorio Promineo: www.promineo.gq.nu.

14-9) Feijóo Samuel. The Knowledge of Juan Without Anything. Signs in the Expression of the People. Saying. Santa Clara. Cuba. Revista Signos. No 14. Year 5, No 2; January-April 1974. p. 56.

150- Emma Cárdenas Acuña. Protocol and Ceremony. In: Group of Authors. Public Relations Manual. Havana. Cuba. Ediciones Logos; 2002. p. 291.

151- Dios Habla Hoy. The Bible with Deuterocanonical Books. Popular Version. Second Edition. Mexico D.F. United Bible Societies; 1987. p. 97.

152- Feijóo Samuel. The Knowledge of Juan Without Anything. Signs in the Expression of the People. Saying. Santa Clara. Cuba. Revista Signos. No 14. Year 5, No 2; January-April 1974. p. 130.

153- Solís José Antonio. Sayings, Proverbs, and Maxims. The Whole Treasure of Popular Wisdom of the Peoples of Spain Within Your Reach. Spain. El Arca de Papel Editores; 2003. p.24.

154- Feijóo Samuel. The Knowledge of Juan Without Anything. Signs in the Expression of the People. Saying. Santa Clara. Cuba. Revista Signos. No 14. Year 5, No 2; January-April 1974. p. 168.

155- Feijóo Samuel. The Knowledge of Juan Without Anything. Signs in the Expression of the People. Saying. Santa Clara. Cuba. Revista Signos. No 14. Year 5, No 2; January-April 1974. p. 177.

156- Flores-Huerta Samuel. Sayings or Proverbs. Thematic Compendium. Mexico: CopIt-arXives; 2016. p. 146.

157- Feijóo Samuel. The Knowledge of Juan Without Anything. Signs in the Expression of the People. Saying. Santa Clara. Cuba. Revista Signos. No 14. Year 5, No 2; January-April 1974. p. 27.

158- Feijóo Samuel. The Knowledge of Juan Without Anything. Signs in the Expression of the People. Saying. Santa Clara. Cuba. Revista Signos. No 14. Year 5, No 2; January-April 1974. p. 200.

159- Valdés Jane Ernesto. Divinatory Sayings of the Caracol and the Odun of Ifá. -In Cuban Santería- Documents for the History and Culture of Osha-Ifá in Cuba. Sayings from (5-5) Oshé tonti Oshé. First Edition: Proyecto Orunmila; 2007. p. 18. Available at:

160- Feijóo Samuel. The Knowledge of Juan Without Anything. Signs in the Expression of the People. Saying. Santa Clara. Cuba. Revista Signos. No 14. Year 5, No 2; January-April 1974. p. 194.

161- Feijóo Samuel. The Knowledge of Juan Without Anything. Signs in the Expression of the People. Saying. Santa Clara. Cuba. Revista Signos. No 14. Year 5, No 2; January-April 1974. p. 114.

162- Solís José Antonio. Sayings, Proverbs, and Maxims. The Whole Treasure of Popular Wisdom of the Peoples of Spain Within Your Reach. Spain. El Arca de Papel Editores; 2003. p.87.

163- Feijóo Samuel. The Knowledge of Juan Without Anything. Signs in the Expression of the People. Saying. Santa Clara. Cuba. Revista Signos. No 14. Year 5, No 2; January-April 1974. p. 54.

164- Solís José Antonio. Sayings, Proverbs, and Maxims. The Whole Treasure of Popular Wisdom of the Peoples of Spain Within Your Reach. Spain. El Arca de Papel Editores; 2003. p.40.

165- Feijóo Samuel. The Knowledge of Juan Without Anything. Signs in the Expression of the People. Saying. Santa Clara. Cuba. Revista Signos. No 14. Year 5, No 2; January-April 1974. p. 104.

166- Quevedo: Taken from "The Author and His Work." Cuban Book Institute, Editorial Pueblo y Educación, Havana, 1974. p. 32.

167- *Feijóo Samuel. The Knowledge of Juan Without Anything. Signs in the Expression of the People. Saying. Santa Clara. Cuba. Revista Signos. No 14. Year 5, No 2; January-April 1974. p. 26.*

168- *Maldonado Felipe CR. Being and Time. Themes of Spain. Classic Spanish Sayings and Other Popular Sayings. Madrid. Spain. Taurus Ediciones S.A.; 1960. p. 15.*

169- *Feijóo Samuel. The Knowledge of Juan Without Anything. Signs in the Expression of the People. Saying. Santa Clara. Cuba. Revista Signos. No 14. Year 5, No 2; January-April 1974. p. 63.*

170- *Solís José Antonio. Sayings, Proverbs, and Maxims. The Whole Treasure of Popular Wisdom of the Peoples of Spain Within Your Reach. Spain. El Arca de Papel Editores; 2003. p. 141.*

171- *Feijóo Samuel. The Knowledge of Juan Without Anything. Signs in the Expression of the People. Saying. Santa Clara. Cuba. Revista Signos. No 14. Year 5, No 2; January-April 1974. p. 197.*

172- *Feijóo Samuel. The Knowledge of Juan Without Anything. Signs in the Expression of the People. Saying. Santa Clara. Cuba. Revista Signos. No 14. Year 5, No 2; January-April 1974. p. 54.*

173- *Feijóo Samuel. The Knowledge of Juan Without Anything. Signs in the Expression of the People. Saying. Santa Clara. Cuba. Revista Signos. No 14. Year 5, No 2; January-April 1974. p. 54.*

174- *Lao Tse. Tao Teh Ching. In: Lin Yutang. Chinese Wisdom. Buenos Aires. Argentina. Colección ACADEMUS. Biblioteca Nueva; 1945. p. 29.*

175- *United Bible Societies. Dios Habla Hoy. The Bible with Deuterocanonical Books. Popular Version. Second Edition. Old Testament. Ecclesiastes. Mexico D.F.: United Bible Societies; 1987. p. 612.*

176- *Maldonado Felipe CR. Being and Time. Themes of Spain. Classic Spanish Sayings and Other Popular Sayings. Madrid. Spain. Taurus Ediciones S.A.; 1960. p. 69.*

177- *Feijóo Samuel. The Knowledge of Juan Without Anything. Signs in the Expression of the People. Saying. Santa Clara. Cuba. Revista Signos. No 14. Year 5, No 2; January-April 1974. p. 151.*

178- *Maldonado Felipe CR. Being and Time. Themes of Spain. Classic Spanish Sayings and Other Popular Sayings. Madrid. Spain. Taurus Ediciones S.A.; 1960. p. 89.*

179- *Feijóo Samuel. From Compliments to Witty Remarks, Oral Folklore of Cuba. Havana. Cuba. Editorial Letras Cubanas; 1981. p. 36.*

180- *Dios Habla Hoy. The Bible with Deuterocanonical Books. Popular Version. Second Edition. Mexico D.F. United Bible Societies; 1987. p. 589.*

181- *Feijóo Samuel. The Knowledge of Juan Without Anything. Signs in the Expression of the People. Saying. Santa Clara. Cuba. Revista Signos. No 14. Year 5, No 2; January-April 1974. p. 178.*

182- *Valdés Jane Ernesto. Divinatory Sayings of the Caracol and the Odun of Ifá. -In Cuban Santería- Documents for the History and Culture of Osha-Ifá in Cuba. Sayings from (6-6) Obara tonti Obara. First Edition: Proyecto Orunmila; 2007. p. 22.*

183- *Valdés Jane Ernesto. Divinatory Sayings of the Caracol and the Odun of Ifá. -In Cuban Santería- Documents for the History and Culture of Osha-Ifá in Cuba. Sayings from (12-4) Eyilá tonti Iroso. First Edition: Proyecto Orunmila; 2007. p. 50.*

184- *Dios Habla Hoy. The Bible with Deuterocanonical Books. Popular Version. Second Edition. Mexico D.F. United Bible Societies; 1987. p. 126.*

185- *Dios Habla Hoy. The Bible with Deuterocanonical Books. Popular Version. Second Edition. Mexico D.F. United Bible Societies; 1987. p. 126.*

186- *Feijóo Samuel. From Compliments to Witty Remarks, Oral Folklore of Cuba. Havana. Cuba. Editorial Letras Cubanas; 1981. p. 24.*

187- *Feijóo Samuel. The Knowledge of Juan Without Anything. Signs in the Expression of the People. Saying. Santa Clara. Cuba. Revista Signos. No 14. Year 5, No 2; January-April 1974. p. 158.*

188- *Valdés Jane Ernesto. Divinatory Sayings of the Caracol and the Odun of Ifá. -In Cuban Santería- Documents for the History and Culture of Osha-Ifá in Cuba. Sayings from (6-6) Obara tonti Obara. First Edition: Proyecto Orunmila; 2007. p. 23.*

189- *Dios Habla Hoy. The Bible with Deuterocanonical Books. Popular Version. Second Edition. Mexico D.F. United Bible Societies; 1987. p. 110.*

190- *Feijóo Samuel. The Knowledge of Juan Without Anything. Signs in the Expression of the People. Saying. Santa Clara. Cuba. Revista Signos. No 14. Year 5, No 2; January-April 1974. p. 76.*

191- *Solís José Antonio. Sayings, Proverbs, and Maxims. The Whole Treasure of Popular Wisdom of the Peoples of Spain Within Your Reach. Spain. El Arca de Papel Editores; 2003. p. 26.*

192- *Feijóo Samuel. The Knowledge of Juan Without Anything. Signs in the Expression of the People. Saying. Santa Clara. Cuba. Revista Signos. No 14. Year 5, No 2; January-April 1974. p. 58.*

193- *Dios Habla Hoy. The Bible with Deuterocanonical Books. Popular Version. Second Edition. Mexico D.F. United Bible Societies; 1987. p. 97.*

194- *Solís José Antonio. Sayings, Proverbs, and Maxims. The Whole Treasure of Popular Wisdom of the Peoples of Spain Within Your Reach. Spain. El Arca de Papel Editores; 2003. p. 51.*

195- *Solís José Antonio. Sayings, Proverbs, and Maxims. The Whole Treasure of Popular Wisdom of the Peoples of Spain Within Your Reach. Spain. El Arca de Papel Editores; 2003. p. 141.*

196- *De Quevedo y Villegas F. In: The Author and His Work. Havana. Cuba. Cuban Book Institute, Editorial Pueblo y Educación; 1974. p. 32.*

197- *Feijóo Samuel. The Knowledge of Juan Without Anything. Signs in the Expression of the People. Saying. Santa Clara. Cuba. Revista Signos. No 14. Year 5, No 2; January-April 1974. p. 14.*

198- *Solís José Antonio. Sayings, Proverbs, and Maxims. The Whole Treasure of Popular Wisdom of the Peoples of Spain Within Your Reach. Spain. El Arca de Papel Editores; 2003. p. 8.*

199- *Flores-Huerta Samuel. Sayings or Proverbs. Thematic Compendium. Mexico: CopIt-arXives; 2016. p. 46. Available at:*

200- *The saying collected by Samuel Flores-Huerta is: "It's no use fighting when love is not mutual." In: Flores-Huerta Samuel. Sayings or Proverbs. Thematic Compendium. Mexico: CopIt-arXives; 2016. p. 45. Available at:*

201- *Álvarez de los Ríos Tomás. The Book of Sayings. Camagüey. Cuba: Editorial Ácana; 2017. p. 20.*

202- *Martí José. Our America. The Prehistoric Chronology of America. In: Complete Works, Vol. VIII. Havana. Cuba. Editorial de Ciencias Sociales; 1991. p. 341.*

203- *Dios Habla Hoy. The Bible with Deuterocanonical Books. Popular Version. Second Edition. Mexico D.F. United Bible Societies; 1987. p. 100.*

204- *The saying collected by Samuel Feijóo was: "He who bends too much shows his backside." In: Feijóo Samuel. The Knowledge of Juan Without Anything. Signs in the Expression of the People. Saying. Santa Clara. Cuba. Revista Signos. No 14. Year 5, No 2; January-April 1974. p. 183.*

205- *One Hundred Proverbs by Mr. Tut-Tut. In: Lin Yutang. Chinese Wisdom. Buenos Aires. Argentina. Colección ACADEMUS. Biblioteca Nueva; 1945. p. 671.*

206- *Franklin Benjamín. Autobiography and Other Writings. Mexico. Editorial Porrua, S.A; 1989. p. 112.*

207- Martí José. *Complete Works. Vol. II. Commemorative edition for the fiftieth anniversary of his death. Havana. Cuba. Editorial Lex; 1946. p. 1846.*

208- Lao Tsé. *Tao Teh Ching. In: Lin Yutang. Chinese Wisdom, Buenos Aires. Argentina. Colección ACADEMUS. Biblioteca Nueva; 1945. p. 63.*

209- Simonov Pavel. *Brain Motivation. Higher Nervous Activity and Scientific Foundations of General Psychology. Moscow. Editorial Mir. 1990. pp. 62, 238.*

210- *A man's sexual attractiveness is closely related to behaviors indicative of social success, suggesting a good position and the ability to satisfy the family's tastes. This image is conveyed, whether true or not, when one is self-confident.*

211- Lao Tsé. *Tao Teh Ching. In: Lin Yutang. Chinese Wisdom. Buenos Aires. Argentina. Colección ACADEMUS. Biblioteca Nueva; 1945. p. 38.*

212- Dios Habla Hoy. *The Bible with Deuterocanonical Books. Popular Version. Second Edition. Mexico D.F. United Bible Societies; 1987. p. 210.*

213- Valdés Jane Ernesto. *Divinatory Sayings of the Caracol and the Odun of Ifá. -In Cuban Santería- Documents for the History and Culture of Osha-Ifá in Cuba. Sayings from (4-15) Iroso tonti Marunlá. First Edition: Proyecto Orunmila; 2007. p. 16.*

214- Valdés Jane Ernesto. *Divinatory Sayings of the Caracol and the Odun of Ifá. -In Cuban Santería- Documents for the History and Culture of Osha-Ifá in Cuba. Sayings from (4-12) Iroso tonti Eyilá. First Edition: Proyecto Orunmila; 2007. p. 16.*

215- Feijóo Samuel. *The Knowledge of Juan Without Anything. Signs in the Expression of the People. Saying. Santa Clara. Cuba. Revista Signos. No 14. Year 5, No 2; January-April 1974. p. 200.*

216- Clavijo Portieles Alberto. *Crisis, Family, and Psychotherapy. Second Edition. Havana. Cuba. Editorial Ciencias Médicas; 2011. p. 167.*

217- *These tensions are due, among other things, to the incursion into the other's inner world, the invasion of the safety distance, or the expectation of a possible rejection.*

218- Solís José Antonio. *Sayings, Proverbs, and Maxims. The Whole Treasure of Popular Wisdom of the Peoples of Spain Within Your Reach. Spain. El Arca de Papel Editores; 2003. p. 49.*

219- Solís José Antonio. *Sayings, Proverbs, and Maxims. The Whole Treasure of Popular Wisdom of the Peoples of Spain Within Your Reach. Spain. El Arca de Papel Editores; 2003. p. 110.*

220- Martí José. *Complete Works. Vol. II. Commemorative edition for the fiftieth anniversary of his death.* Havana. Cuba. Editorial Lex; 1946. p. 1846.

221- Erasmus Desiderius. *Complete Works.* Madrid. Spain. Editorial Aguilar; 1956. p. 571.

222- Dios Habla Hoy. *The Bible with Deuterocanonical Books. Popular Version. Second Edition.* Mexico D.F. United Bible Societies; 1987. p. 593.

223- De Valbuena D. M. *Complete Works of Marcus Tullius Cicero. Vol. IV.* Madrid. Spain. Librería de la Viuda de Hernando y C; 1893. p. 114.

224- Feijóo Samuel. *The Knowledge of Juan Without Anything. Signs in the Expression of the People. Saying.* Santa Clara. Cuba. Revista Signos. No 14. Year 5, No 2; January-April 1974. p. 87.

225- Feijóo Samuel. *The Knowledge of Juan Without Anything. Signs in the Expression of the People. Saying.* Santa Clara. Cuba. Revista Signos. No 14. Year 5, No 2; January-April 1974. p. 200.

226- The saying compiled by Samuel Feijóo is: "Don't prepare the spear when the antelope is in front of you." *Feijóo Samuel. The Knowledge of Juan Without Anything. Signs in the Expression of the People. Saying.* Santa Clara. Cuba. Revista Signos. No 14. Year 5, No 2; January-April 1974. p. 210.

227- Feijóo Samuel. *The Knowledge of Juan Without Anything. Signs in the Expression of the People. Saying.* Santa Clara. Cuba. Revista Signos. No 14. Year 5, No 2; January-April 1974. p. 203.

228- Martí José. *De Patria, New York. March 14, 1892. Our Ideas. In: Complete Works, Vol. I.* Havana. Cuba. Editorial de Ciencias Sociales; 1991. p. 316.

229- Confucius. *In: Lin Yutang. The Wisdom of Confucius.* Buenos Aires. Argentina. Ediciones Siglo Veinte; 1952. p. 142.

230- Masters WH, Johnson VE, Kolodny RC. *Human Sexuality.* Havana. Cuba. Editorial Científico Técnica; 1987. p. 375.

231- Dios Habla Hoy. *The Bible with Deuterocanonical Books. Popular Version. Second Edition.* Mexico D.F. United Bible Societies; 1987. p. 97.

232- Dios Habla Hoy. *The Bible with Deuterocanonical Books. Popular Version. Second Edition.* Mexico D.F. United Bible Societies; 1987. p. 94.

233- Dios Habla Hoy. *The Bible with Deuterocanonical Books. Popular Version. Second Edition.* Mexico D.F. United Bible Societies; 1987. p. 97.

234- Dios Habla Hoy. *The Bible with Deuterocanonical Books. Popular Version. Second Edition.* Mexico D.F. United Bible Societies; 1987. p. 604.

235- *Dios Habla Hoy. The Bible with Deuterocanonical Books. Popular Version. Second Edition. Mexico D.F. United Bible Societies; 1987. p. 607.*

236- *Martí José. Notebooks. In: Complete Works, Vol. XXI. Havana. Cuba. Editorial de Ciencias Sociales; 1991. p. 107.*

237- *Lin Yutang. Chinese Wisdom. Buenos Aires. Argentina. Colección ACADEMUS. Biblioteca Nueva; 1945. p. 671.*

238- *Feijóo Samuel. The Knowledge of Juan Without Anything. Signs in the Expression of the People. Saying. Santa Clara. Cuba. Revista Signos. No 14. Year 5, No 2; January-April 1974. p. 201.*

239- *Feijóo Samuel. From Compliments to Witty Remarks, Oral Folklore of Cuba. Havana. Cuba. Editorial Letras Cubanas; 1981. p. 25.*

240- *Feijóo Samuel. The Knowledge of Juan Without Anything. Signs in the Expression of the People. Saying. Santa Clara. Cuba. Revista Signos. No 14. Year 5, No 2; January-April 1974. p. 110.*

241- *Feijóo Samuel. The Knowledge of Juan Without Anything. Signs in the Expression of the People. Saying. Santa Clara. Cuba. Revista Signos. No 14. Year 5, No 2; January-April 1974. p. 156.*

242- *Solís José Antonio. Sayings, Proverbs, and Maxims. The Whole Treasure of Popular Wisdom of the Peoples of Spain Within Your Reach. Spain. El Arca de Papel Editores; 2003. p. 21.*

243- *Solarte Mejia Lidardo. Sayings and Proverbs. Bogotá. Colombia. Editora Dosmil; 1979. p. 34.*

244- *Solís José Antonio. Sayings, Proverbs, and Maxims. The Whole Treasure of Popular Wisdom of the Peoples of Spain Within Your Reach. Spain. El Arca de Papel Editores; 2003. p. 23.*

245- *Flores-Huerta Samuel. Sayings or Proverbs. Thematic Compendium. Mexico: CopIt-arXives; 2016. p. 146.*

246- *Feijóo Samuel. The Knowledge of Juan Without Anything. Signs in the Expression of the People. Saying. Santa Clara. Cuba. Revista Signos. No 14. Year 5, No 2; January-April 1974. p. 55.*

247- *Solís José Antonio. Sayings, Proverbs, and Maxims. The Whole Treasure of Popular Wisdom of the Peoples of Spain Within Your Reach. Spain. El Arca de Papel Editores; 2003. p. 41.*

248- *Feijóo Samuel. The Knowledge of Juan Without Anything. Signs in the Expression of the People. Saying. Santa Clara. Cuba. Revista Signos. No 14. Year 5, No 2; January-April 1974. p. 52.*

249- Feijóo Samuel. *The Knowledge of Juan Without Anything. Signs in the Expression of the People. Saying.* Santa Clara. Cuba. Revista Signos. No 14. Year 5, No 2; January-April 1974. p. 63.

250- Martí José. *Notebooks. In: Complete Works, Vol. XXI.* Havana. Cuba. Editorial de Ciencias Sociales; 1991. p. 107.

251- Valdés Jane Ernesto. *Divinatory Sayings of the Caracol and the Odun of Ifá. -In Cuban Santería- Documents for the History and Culture of Osha-Ifá in Cuba. Sayings from (11-14) Ojuani tonti Merinlá and Ojuani Tanshela.* First Edition: Proyecto Orunmila; 2007. p. 48 and 90.

252- Solís José Antonio. *Sayings, Proverbs, and Maxims. The Whole Treasure of Popular Wisdom of the Peoples of Spain Within Your Reach.* Spain. El Arca de Papel Editores; 2003. p. 89.

253- Solís José Antonio. *Sayings, Proverbs, and Maxims. The Whole Treasure of Popular Wisdom of the Peoples of Spain Within Your Reach.* Spain. El Arca de Papel Editores; 2003. p. 153.

254- Solís José Antonio. *Sayings, Proverbs, and Maxims. The Whole Treasure of Popular Wisdom of the Peoples of Spain Within Your Reach.* Spain. El Arca de Papel Editores; 2003. p. 91.

255- Sintes Pros Jorge. *Dictionary of Aphorisms, Proverbs, and Sayings.* Barcelona. Spain. Editorial Sintes; 1954. p. 276.

256- Solís José Antonio. *Sayings, Proverbs, and Maxims. The Whole Treasure of Popular Wisdom.* Spain. El Arca de Papel Editores; 2003. p. 70.

257- Solís José Antonio. *Sayings, Proverbs, and Maxims. The Whole Treasure of Popular Wisdom of the Peoples of Spain Within Your Reach.* Spain. El Arca de Papel Editores; 2003. p. 82.

258- Sintes Pros Jorge. *Dictionary of Aphorisms, Proverbs, and Sayings.* Barcelona. Spain. Editorial Sintes; 1954. p. 235.

259- Sintes Pros Jorge. *Dictionary of Aphorisms, Proverbs, and Sayings.* Barcelona. Spain. Editorial Sintes; 1954. p. 103.

260- Solís José Antonio. *Sayings, Proverbs, and Maxims.* Spain. El Arca de Papel Editores; 2003. p. 35.

261- Ovidio Nasón P. *The Art of Love.* Madrid. Spain. EDIMAT LIBROS. S.A.; 2006. p. 56.

262- Valdés Jane Ernesto. *Divinatory Sayings of the Caracol and the Odun of Ifá. -In Cuban Santería- Documents for the History and Culture of Osha-Ifá in Cuba. Sayings from (5-8) Oshé tonti Eyeúnle and Oshe Nilogbe.* First Edition: Proyecto Orunmila; 2007. p. 18 and 121. Available at URL:

263- Solís José Antonio. *Sayings, Proverbs, and Maxims. The Whole Treasure of Popular Wisdom of the Peoples of Spain Within Your Reach.* Spain. El Arca de Papel Editores; 2003. p. 112.

264- The saying collected by Tomás Álvarez de los Ríos is: "Absence and saltwater erase love." In: Álvarez de los Ríos Tomás. *The Book of Sayings.* Camagüey. Cuba: Editorial Ácana; 2017. p. 68.

265- Feijóo Samuel. *The Knowledge of Juan Without Anything. Signs in the Expression of the People. Saying.* Santa Clara. Cuba. Revista Signos. No 14. Year 5, No 2; January-April 1974. p. 202.

266- Álvarez de los Ríos Tomás. *The Book of Sayings.* Camagüey. Cuba: Editorial Ácana; 2017. p. 21.

267- Sintes Pros Jorge. *Dictionary of Aphorisms, Proverbs, and Sayings.* Barcelona. Spain. Editorial Sintes; 1954. p. 290.

268- Maldonado Felipe CR. *Being and Time. Spanish Themes. Classical Spanish Refranero and Other Popular Sayings.* Madrid. Spain. Taurus Ediciones S.A.; 1960. p. 44.

269- Feijóo Samuel. *The Knowledge of Juan Without Anything. Signs in the Expression of the People. Saying.* Santa Clara. Cuba. Revista Signos. No 14. Year 5, No 2; January-April 1974. p. 64.

270- Confucius in: Lin Yutang. *The Wisdom of Confucius.* Buenos Aires. Argentina. Ediciones Siglo Veinte; 1952. p. 174.

271- Valdés Jane Ernesto. *Divinatory Sayings of the Caracol and the Odun of Ifá. -In Cuban Santería- Documents for the History and Culture of Osha-Ifá in Cuba. Sayings from (9-3) Osá tonti Ogundá.* First Edition: Proyecto Orunmila; 2007. p. 36. Available at URL:

272- Solís José Antonio. *Sayings, Proverbs, and Maxims. The Whole Treasure of Popular Wisdom of the Peoples of Spain Within Your Reach.* Spain. El Arca de Papel Editores; 2003. p. 93.

273- Flores-Huerta Samuel. *Sayings or Proverbs. Thematic Compendium.* Mexico: CopIt-arXives; 2016. p. 146. Available at URL:

274- Flores-Huerta Samuel. *Sayings or Proverbs. Thematic Compendium.* Mexico: CopIt-arXives; 2016. p. 146. Available at URL:

275- Solís José Antonio. *Sayings, Proverbs, and Maxims. The Whole Treasure of Popular Wisdom of the Peoples of Spain Within Your Reach.* Spain. El Arca de Papel Editores; 2003. p. 89.

276- Solís José Antonio. *Sayings, Proverbs, and Maxims. The Whole Treasure of Popular Wisdom of the Peoples of Spain Within Your Reach.* Spain. El Arca de Papel Editores; 2003. p. 109.

277- Valdés Jane Ernesto. *Divinatory Sayings of the Caracol and the Odun of Ifá. -In Cuban Santería- Documents for the History and Culture of Osha-Ifá in Cuba. Sayings from (1-5) Okana tonti Oshé. First Edition: Proyecto Orunmila; 2007. p. 2. Available at URL:*

278- Flores-Huerta Samuel. *Sayings or Proverbs. Thematic Compendium. Mexico. CopIt-arXives; 2016. p. 49. Available at URL:*

279- Solís José Antonio. *Sayings, Proverbs, and Maxims. The Whole Treasure of Popular Wisdom of the Peoples of Spain Within Your Reach. Spain. El Arca de Papel Editores; 2003. p. 93.*

280- *God Speaks Today. The Bible with Deuterocanonicals. Popular Version. Second Edition. Mexico City. United Bible Societies; 1987. p. 94.*

281- Feijóo Samuel. *The Knowledge of Juan Without Anything. Signs in the Expression of the People. Saying. Santa Clara. Cuba. Revista Signos. No 14. Year 5, No 2; January-April 1974. p. 143.*

282- *God Speaks Today. The Bible with Deuterocanonicals. Popular Version. Second Edition. Mexico City. United Bible Societies; 1987. p. 591.*

283- Feijóo Samuel. *The Knowledge of Juan Without Anything. Signs in the Expression of the People. Saying. Santa Clara. Cuba. Revista Signos. No 14. Year 5, No 2; January-April 1974. p. 191.*

284- Feijóo Samuel. *The Knowledge of Juan Without Anything. Signs in the Expression of the People. Saying. Santa Clara. Cuba. Revista Signos. No 14. Year 5, No 2; January-April 1974. p. 195.*

285- Feijóo Samuel. *The Knowledge of Juan Without Anything. Signs in the Expression of the People. Saying. Santa Clara. Cuba. Revista Signos. No 14. Year 5, No 2; January-April 1974. p. 67.*

286- Feijóo Samuel. *The Knowledge of Juan Without Anything. Signs in the Expression of the People. Saying. Santa Clara. Cuba. Revista Signos. No 14. Year 5, No 2; January-April 1974. p. 195.*

287- Martí José. *General Epistolary. To His Sister Amelia. In: Complete Works, Vol. XX. Havana. Cuba. Editorial de Ciencias Sociales; 1991. p. 287.*

288- Valdés Jane Ernesto. *Divinatory Sayings of the Caracol and the Odun of Ifá. -In Cuban Santería- Documents for the History and Culture of Osha-Ifá in Cuba. Sayings from (8-5) Eyeúnle tonti Oshé and Ogbe She. First Edition: Proyecto Orunmila; 2007. p. 31 and 74. Available at URL:*

289- Valdés Jane Ernesto. *Divinatory Sayings of the Caracol and the Odun of Ifá. -In Cuban Santería- Documents for the History and Culture of Osha-Ifá in Cuba. Sayings from (12-2) Eyilá tonti Eyioko and Otrupon Yekun. First Edition: Proyecto Orunmila; 2007. p. 49 and 111. Available at URL:*

290- Flores-Huerta Samuel. Sayings or Proverbs. Thematic Compendium. Mexico: CopIt-arXives; 2016. p. 30. Available at URL:

291- Valdés Jane Ernesto. Divinatory Sayings of the Caracol and the Odun of Ifá. -In Cuban Santería- Documents for the History and Culture of Osha-Ifá in Cuba. Sayings from (15-6) Marunlá tonti Obara. First Edition: Proyecto Orunmila; 2007. p. 61. Available at URL:

292- Feijóo Samuel. The Knowledge of Juan Without Anything. Signs in the Expression of the People. Saying. Santa Clara. Cuba. Revista Signos. No 14. Year 5, No 2; January-April 1974. p. 158.

293- Sintes Pros Jorge. Dictionary of Aphorisms, Proverbs, and Sayings. Barcelona. Spain. Editorial Sintes; 1954. p. 85.

294- Martí José. Letter to José Dolores Poyo, New York, July 7, 1894. In: Complete Works, Vol. III. Havana. Cuba. Editorial de Ciencias Sociales; 1991. p. 225.

295- Feijóo Samuel. The Knowledge of Juan Without Anything. Signs in the Expression of the People. Saying. Santa Clara. Cuba. Revista Signos. No 14. Year 5, No 2; January-April 1974. p. 186.

296- God Speaks Today. The Bible with Deuterocanonicals. Popular Version. Second Edition. Mexico City. United Bible Societies; 1987. p. 612.

297- Lao Tse. Tao Teh Ching. In: Lin Yutang. Chinese Wisdom. Buenos Aires. Argentina. Colección ACADEMUS. Biblioteca Nueva; 1945. p. 29.

298- Feijóo Samuel. The Knowledge of Juan Without Anything. Signs in the Expression of the People. Saying. Santa Clara. Cuba. Revista Signos. No 14. Year 5, No 2; January-April 1974. p. 92.

299- Solís José Antonio. Sayings, Proverbs, and Maxims. The Whole Treasure of Popular Wisdom of the Peoples of Spain Within Your Reach. Spain. El Arca de Papel Editores; 2003. p. 120.

300- Solís José Antonio. Sayings, Proverbs, and Maxims. The Whole Treasure of Popular Wisdom of the Peoples of Spain Within Your Reach. Spain. El Arca de Papel Editores; 2003. p. 150.

301- Feijóo Samuel. The Knowledge of Juan Without Anything. Signs in the Expression of the People. Saying. Santa Clara. Cuba. Revista Signos. No 14. Year 5, No 2; January-April 1974. p. 200.

302- Feijóo Samuel. The Knowledge of Juan Without Anything. Signs in the Expression of the People. Proverb. Santa Clara. Cuba. Signos Magazine. No 14. Year 5, No 2; January-April 1974. p. 151.

303- Valdés Jane Ernesto. Divinatory Proverbs of the Snail and the Oduns of Ifá. -In Cuban Santeria- Documents for the History and Culture of Osha-Ifa in Cuba. Proverbs from (9-1) Osá tonti Okana. First Edition: Proyecto Orunmila; 2007. p. 35. Available at URL:

304- Valdés Jane Ernesto. Divinatory Proverbs of the Snail and the Oduns of Ifá. -In Cuban Santeria- Documents for the History and Culture of Osha-Ifa in Cuba. Proverbs from (15-14) Marunlá tonti Merinlá. First Edition: Proyecto Orunmila; 2007. p. 62. Available at URL:

305- Valdés Jane Ernesto. Divinatory Proverbs of the Snail and the Oduns of Ifá. -In Cuban Santeria- Documents for the History and Culture of Osha-Ifa in Cuba. Proverbs from (4-1) Iroso tonti Okana. First Edition: Proyecto Orunmila; 2007. p. 13. Available at URL:

306- United Bible Societies. God Speaks Today. The Bible with Deuterocanonical Books. Deuterocanonical Books. Ecclesiasticus. Popular Version. Second Edition. Mexico City: United Bible Societies; 1987. p. 96.

307- Flores-Huerta Samuel. Sayings or Proverbs. Thematic Compendium. Mexico. CopIt-arXives; 2016. p. 99. Available at URL:

308- Solís José Antonio. Proverbs, sayings, sayings, and sentences. The entire treasure of popular wisdom from the towns of Spain at your disposal. Spain. El Arca de Papel Editores; 2003. p. 138.

309- The proverb collected by José Antonio Solís is: "A timely retreat is a victory." In: Solís José Antonio. Proverbs, sayings, sayings, and sentences. The entire treasure of popular wisdom from the towns of Spain at your disposal. Spain. El Arca de Papel Editores; 2003. p. 154.

310- Solís José Antonio. Proverbs, sayings, sayings, and sentences. The entire treasure of popular wisdom from the towns of Spain at your disposal. Spain. El Arca de Papel Editores; 2003. p. 109.

311- Solís José Antonio. Proverbs, sayings, sayings, and sentences. The entire treasure of popular wisdom from the towns of Spain at your disposal. Spain. El Arca de Papel Editores; 2003. p.42.

312- Feijóo Samuel. The Knowledge of Juan Without Anything. Signs in the Expression of the People. Proverb. Santa Clara. Cuba. Signos Magazine. No 14. Year 5, No 2; January-April 1974. p. 110.

313- Feijóo Samuel. The Knowledge and Singing of Juan Without Anything. Havana City. Cuba. Letras Cubanas Publishing House; 1984. p. 197.

314- Feijóo Samuel. The Knowledge of Juan Without Anything. Signs in the Expression of the People. Proverb. Santa Clara. Cuba. Signos Magazine. No 14. Year 5, No 2; January-April 1974. p. 114.

315- Valdés Jane Ernesto. Divinatory Proverbs of the Snail and the Oduns of Ifá. -In Cuban Santeria- Documents for the History and Culture of Osha-Ifa *in Cuba. Proverbs from (12-8) Eyilá tonti Eyeúnl. First Edition: Proyecto Orunmila; 2007. p. 51. Available at URL:*

316- God Speaks Today. The Bible with Deuterocanonical Books. Popular Version. Second Edition. Mexico City: United Bible Societies; 1987. p.598.

317- God Speaks Today. The Bible with Deuterocanonical Books. Popular Version. Second Edition. Mexico City: United Bible Societies; 1987. pp.596-597.

318- God Speaks Today. The Bible with Deuterocanonical Books. Popular Version. Second Edition. Mexico City: United Bible Societies; 1987. p.596.

319- Feijóo Samuel. The Knowledge of Juan Without Anything. Signs in the Expression of the People. Proverb. Santa Clara. Cuba. Signos Magazine. No 14. Year 5, No 2; January-April 1974. p. 75.

320- Feijóo Samuel. The Knowledge of Juan Without Anything. Signs in the Expression of the People. Proverb. Santa Clara. Cuba. Signos Magazine. No 14. Year 5, No 2; January-April 1974. p. 76.

321- Solís José Antonio. Proverbs, sayings, sayings, and sentences. The entire treasure of popular wisdom from the towns of Spain at your disposal. La Coruña. Spain: El Arca de Papel Editores; 2003. p.15.

322- Flores-Huerta Samuel. Sayings or Proverbs. Thematic Compendium. Mexico. CopIt-arXives; 2016. p.155. Available at URL:

323- Feijóo Samuel. The Knowledge of Juan Without Anything. Signs in the Expression of the People. Proverb. Santa Clara. Cuba. Signos Magazine. No 14. Year 5, No 2; January-April 1974. p. 133.

324- God Speaks Today. The Bible with Deuterocanonical Books. Popular Version. Second Edition. Mexico City: United Bible Societies; 1987. p.595.

325- The proverb collected by José Antonio Solís is: Rabiar y malcasar todo es a la par. In: Solís José Antonio. Proverbs, sayings, sayings, and sentences. The entire treasure of popular wisdom. Spain. El Arca de Papel Editores; 2003. p.137.

326- Maldonado Felipe CR. Being and Time. Topics of Spain. Classical Spanish Refranero and Other Popular Sayings. Madrid. Spain. Taurus Ediciones S.A.; 1960. p. 139.

327- The importance of a correct choice of whom to court, and not to start or stop a courtship if we evaluate that there is a lack of compatibility or very undesirable qualities in the other person, is treated in detail in the second chapter.

328- Solís José Antonio. *Proverbs, sayings, sayings, and sentences. The entire treasure of popular wisdom.* Spain. El Arca de Papel Editores; 2003. p.102.

329- Álvarez de los Ríos Tomás. *The Book of Proverbs.* Camagüey. Cuba: Editorial Ácana; 2017. p. 57.

330- Feijóo Samuel. *The Knowledge of Juan Without Anything. Signs in the Expression of the People. Proverb.* Santa Clara. Cuba. Signos Magazine. No 14. Year 5, No 2; January-April 1974, p. 156.

331- Feijóo Samuel. *The Knowledge of Juan Without Anything. Signs in the Expression of the People. Proverb.* Santa Clara. Cuba. Signos Magazine. No 14. Year 5, No 2; January-April 1974, p. 153.

332- *Chinese Aphorisms. In Lin Yutang. Chinese Wisdom.* Buenos Aires. Argentina. ACADEMUS Collection. Biblioteca Nueva; 1945. p. 595.

333- Vishnu Sarma. *Panchatantra.* Havana City. Cuba. Editorial Arte y Literatura; 1989. p. 62.

334- Sintes Pros Jorge. *Dictionary of Aphorisms, Proverbs, and Sayings.* Barcelona. Spain. Editorial Sintes; 1954. p. 103.

335- Sintes Pros Jorge. *Dictionary of Aphorisms, Proverbs, and Sayings.* Barcelona. Spain. Editorial Sintes; 1954. p. 85.

336- Feijóo Samuel. *The Knowledge of Juan Without Anything. Signs in the Expression of the People. Proverb.* Santa Clara. Cuba. Signos Magazine. No 14. Year 5, No 2; January-April 1974. p. 51.

337- Feijóo Samuel. *The Knowledge of Juan Without Anything. Signs in the Expression of the People. Proverb.* Santa Clara. Cuba. Signos Magazine. No 14. Year 5, No 2; January-April 1974. p. 18.

338- *The proverb collected by Samuel Feijóo is: "It never rained that it didn't clear up." In: Feijóo Samuel. From the Compliment to the Sayings, Oral Folklore of Cuba.* Havana City. Cuba. Letras Cubanas Publishing House; 1981. p. 27.

339- *"Racha" is used in naval terminology as a brief gust of wind. Generally, it is used as a period, always short, of good or bad fortune in any activity.*

340- Chuang Tzu. *The Leveling of All Things. In: Lin Yutang. Chinese Wisdom.* Buenos Aires. Argentina. ACADEMUS Collection. Biblioteca Nueva; 1945. p. 79.

341- Chuang Tzu. *Autumn Floods. In Lin Yutang. Chinese Wisdom.* Buenos Aires. Argentina. ACADEMUS Collection. Biblioteca Nueva; 1945. p. 137.

342- *A Hundred Proverbs by Mr. Tut-Tut. In: Lin Yutang. Chinese Wisdom. Buenos Aires. Argentina. ACADEMUS Collection. Biblioteca Nueva; 1945. p. 593.*

343- *Sintes Pros Jorge. Dictionary of Aphorisms, Proverbs, and Sayings. Barcelona. Spain. Editorial Sintes; 1954. p. 291.*

344- *Feijóo Samuel. The Knowledge of Juan Without Anything. Signs in the Expression of the People. Proverb. Santa Clara. Cuba. Signos Magazine. No 14. Year 5, No 2; January-April 1974. p. 52.*

345- *Sintes Pros Jorge. Dictionary of Aphorisms, Proverbs, and Sayings. Barcelona. Spain. Editorial Sintes; 1954. p. 28.*

346- *Flores-Huerta Samuel. Sayings or Proverbs. Thematic Compendium. Mexico. CopIt-arXives; 2016. p. 46. Available at URL:*

347- *Solís José Antonio. Proverbs, Sayings, and Sentences. The Entire Treasure of Popular Wisdom from the Towns of Spain at Your Disposal. Spain. El Arca de Papel Editores; 2003. p. 21.*

348- *Sintes Pros Jorge. Dictionary of Aphorisms, Proverbs, and Sayings. Barcelona. Spain. Editorial Sintes; 1954. p. 76.*

349- *Sintes Pros Jorge. Dictionary of Aphorisms, Proverbs, and Sayings. Barcelona. Spain. Editorial Sintes; 1954. p. 247.*

350- *Solís José Antonio. Proverbs, Sayings, and Sentences. The Entire Treasure of Popular Wisdom from the Towns of Spain at Your Disposal. Spain. El Arca de Papel Editores; 2003. p. 148.*

351- *Flores-Huerta Samuel. Sayings or Proverbs. Thematic Compendium. Mexico: CopIt-arXives; 2016. p. 46. Available at URL:*

352- *Solís José Antonio. Proverbs, Sayings, and Sentences. The Entire Treasure of Popular Wisdom from the Towns of Spain at Your Disposal. Spain. El Arca de Papel Editores; 2003. p. 23.*

353- *Valdés Jane Ernesto. Divinatory Proverbs of the Snail and the Oduns of Ifá. -In Cuban Santeria- Documents for the History and Culture of Osha-Ifa in Cuba. Proverbs from (4-7) Iroso tonti Odí. First Edition: Proyecto Orunmila; 2007. p. 14. Available at URL:*

354- *Feijóo Samuel. The Knowledge of Juan Without Anything. Signs in the Expression of the People. Proverb. Santa Clara. Cuba. Signos Magazine. No 14. Year 5, No 2; January-April 1974. p. 137.*

355- *Feijóo Samuel. The Knowledge of Juan Without Anything. Signs in the Expression of the People. Proverb. Santa Clara. Cuba. Signos Magazine. No 14. Year 5, No 2; January-April 1974. p. 53.*

356- Valdés Jane Ernesto. *Divinatory Proverbs of the Snail and the Oduns of Ifá. -In Cuban Santeria- Documents for the History and Culture of Osha-Ifa in Cuba. Proverbs from (12-16) Eyilá tonti Merindilogún. First Edition: Proyecto Orunmila; 2007. p. 53. Available at URL:*

357- Valdés Jane Ernesto. *Divinatory Proverbs of the Snail and the Oduns of Ifá. -In Cuban Santeria- Documents for the History and Culture of Osha-Ifa in Cuba. Proverbs from (12-6) Eyilá tonti Obar. First Edition: Proyecto Orunmila; 2007. p. 50. Available at URL:*

358- Feijóo Samuel. *The Knowledge of Juan Without Anything. Signs in the Expression of the People. Proverb. Santa Clara. Cuba. Signos Magazine. No 14. Year 5, No 2; January-April 1974. p. 52.*

359- Feijóo Samuel. *From the Compliment to the Sayings, Oral Folklore of Cuba. Havana City. Cuba. Letras Cubanas Publishing House; 1981. p. 28.*

360- Seneca. *In: Sintes Pros Jorge. Great Dictionary of Famous Phrases. Vol. III. Barcelona. Spain. Editorial Sintes; 1960. p. 267.*

361- Feijóo Samuel. *The Knowledge of Juan Without Anything. Signs in the Expression of the People. Proverb. Santa Clara. Cuba. Signos Magazine. No 14. Year 5, No 2; January-April 1974, p. 195.*

362- Sintes Pros Jorge. *Dictionary of Aphorisms, Proverbs, and Sayings. Barcelona. Spain. Editorial Sintes; 1954. p. 234.*

363- Feijóo Samuel. *The Knowledge of Juan Without Anything. Signs in the Expression of the People. Proverb. Santa Clara. Cuba. Signos Magazine. No 14. Year 5, No 2; January-April 1974. p. 127.*

364- Sintes Pros Jorge. *Dictionary of Aphorisms, Proverbs, and Sayings. Barcelona. Spain. Editorial Sintes; 1954. p. 292.*

365- Martí José. *The Soul of the Revolution and the Duty of Cuba in America. In: Complete Works, Vol. III. Havana. Cuba. Editorial de Ciencias Sociales; 1991. p. 142.*

366- Feijóo Samuel. *The Knowledge of Juan Without Anything. Signs in the Expression of the People. Proverb. Santa Clara. Cuba. Signos Magazine. No 14. Year 5, No 2; January-April 1974. p. 86.*

367- Feijóo Samuel. *From the Compliment to the Sayings, Oral Folklore of Cuba. Havana City. Cuba. Letras Cubanas Publishing House; 1981. p. 59.*

368- Maldonado Felipe CR. *Being and Time. Topics from Spain. Classical Spanish Refranero and Other Popular Sayings. Madrid. Spain. Taurus Ediciones S.A.; 1960. p. 102.*

369- Solís José Antonio. *Proverbs, Sayings, and Sentences. The Entire Treasure of Popular Wisdom. Spain. El Arca de Papel Editores; 2003. p. 21.*

370- *God Speaks Today. The Bible with Deuterocanonicals. Popular Version. Second Edition. Mexico City. United Bible Societies; 1987. p. 598.*

371- *Seneca. In: Sintes Pros Jorge. Great Dictionary of Famous Phrases. Vol. II. Barcelona. Spain. Editorial Sintes; 1960. p. 396.*

372- *Seneca. In: Sintes Pros Jorge. Great Dictionary of Famous Phrases. Vol. III. Barcelona. Spain. Editorial Sintes; 1960. p. 302.*

373- *Graf A. In: Sintes Pros Jorge. Great Dictionary of Famous Phrases. Vol. III. Barcelona. Spain. Editorial Sintes; 1960. p. 298.*

374- *Solís José Antonio. Proverbs, Sayings, and Sentences. The Entire Treasure of Popular Wisdom from the Towns of Spain at Your Disposal. Spain. El Arca de Papel Editores; 2003. p. 98.*

375- *Feijóo Samuel. The Knowledge of Juan Without Anything. Signs in the Expression of the People. Proverb. Santa Clara. Cuba. Signos Magazine. No 14. Year 5, No 2; January-April 1974. p. 156.*

376- *The proverb collected by José Antonio Solís is: "Orchard, woman, and mill, want continuous use." In: Solís José Antonio. Proverbs, Sayings, and Sentences. The Entire Treasure of Popular Wisdom. Spain. El Arca de Papel Editores; 2003. p. 77.*

377- *Martí José. Notebooks. In: Complete Works, Vol. XXI. Havana. Cuba. Editorial de Ciencias Sociales; 1991. p. 130.*

378- *Martí José. Notebooks. In: Complete Works, Vol. XXI. Havana. Cuba. Editorial de Ciencias Sociales; 1991. p. 129.*

379- *Martí José. Notebooks. In: Complete Works, Vol. XXI. Havana. Cuba. Editorial de Ciencias Sociales; 1991. p. 130.*

380- *Martí José. Notebooks. In: Complete Works, Vol. XXI. Havana. Cuba. Editorial de Ciencias Sociales; 1991. p. 130.*

381- *Sintes Pros Jorge. Dictionary of Aphorisms, Proverbs, and Sayings. Barcelona. Spain. Editorial Sintes; 1954. p. 285.*

382- *Sintes Pros Jorge. Dictionary of Aphorisms, Proverbs, and Sayings. Barcelona. Spain. Editorial Sintes; 1954. p. 99.*

383- *Valdés Jane Ernesto. Divinatory Proverbs of the Snail and the Oduns of Ifá. -In Cuban Santeria- Documents for the History and Culture of Osha-Ifa in Cuba. Proverbs from (4-4) Iroso tonti Iroso. First Edition: Proyecto Orunmila; 2007. p. 14. Available at URL:*

384- *Valdés Jane Ernesto. Divinatory Proverbs of the Snail and the Oduns of Ifá. -In Cuban Santeria- Documents for the History and Culture of Osha-Ifa in Cuba. Proverbs from (6-15) Obara tonti Marunlá. First Edition: Proyecto Orunmila; 2007. p. 24. Available at URL:*

385- Feijóo Samuel. The Knowledge of Juan Without Anything. Signs in the Expression of the People. Proverb. Santa Clara. Cuba. Signos Magazine. No 14. Year 5, No 2; January-April 1974. p. 200.

386- Feijóo Samuel. The Knowledge of Juan Without Anything. Signs in the Expression of the People. Proverb. Santa Clara. Cuba. Signos Magazine. No 14. Year 5, No 2; January-April 1974. p. 183.

387- Feijóo Samuel. The Knowledge of Juan Without Anything. Signs in the Expression of the People. Proverb. Santa Clara. Cuba. Signos Magazine. No 14. Year 5, No 2; January-April 1974. p. 146.

388- Solís José Antonio. Proverbs, Sayings, and Sentences. The Entire Treasure of Popular Wisdom from the Towns of Spain at Your Disposal. Spain. El Arca de Papel Editores; 2003. p. 127.

389- Feijóo Samuel. The Knowledge of Juan Without Anything. Signs in the Expression of the People. Proverb. Santa Clara. Cuba. Signos Magazine. No 14. Year 5, No 2; January-April 1974. p. 163.

390- God Speaks Today. The Bible with Deuterocanonicals. Popular Version. Second Edition. Mexico City. United Bible Societies; 1987. p. 612.

391- The proverb collected by Jorge Sintes Pros is: "Abundance brings weariness." In: Sintes Pros Jorge. Dictionary of Aphorisms, Proverbs, and Sayings. Barcelona. Spain. Editorial Sintes; 1954. p. 18.

392- The proverb collected by Tomás Álvarez de los Ríos is: "It's as bad to fall short as to overshoot." In: Álvarez de los Ríos Tomás. The Book of Proverbs. Camagüey. Cuba: Editorial Ácana; 2017. p. 108.

393- Feijóo Samuel. The Knowledge of Juan Without Anything. Signs in the Expression of the People. Proverb. Santa Clara. Cuba. Signos Magazine. No 14. Year 5, No 2; January-April 1974. p. 147.

394- Feijóo Samuel. The Knowledge of Juan Without Anything. Signs in the Expression of the People. Proverb. Santa Clara. Cuba. Signos Magazine. No 14. Year 5, No 2; January-April 1974. p. 101.

395- Álvarez de los Ríos Tomás. The Book of Proverbs. Camagüey. Cuba: Editorial Ácana; 2017. p. 53.

396- Solís José Antonio. Proverbs, Sayings, and Sentences. The Entire Treasure of Popular Wisdom from the Towns of Spain at Your Disposal. Spain. El Arca de Papel Editores; 2003. p. 123.

397- Nowadays, it is increasingly common to see women celebrating male beauty in extraordinarily original ways.

~~~

AUTHOR INFORMATION

Arturo José Sánchez Hernández, born in Havana in 1970, is a physician specializing in Comprehensive General Medicine and Psychiatry. He has an extensive professional and academic career, supported by several publications focused on ethics and the theory of values.

With outstanding expertise in sexuality and psychotherapy for couples and families, Dr. Sánchez Hernández has dedicated part of his career to exploring these areas of mental health. He also stands out as the author of self-help and personal growth books, where proverbs and images play a central role.

Currently, he resides in Maun, Botswana, where he works as a psychiatrist at Letsholathebe II Memorial Hospital. His commitment to mental health and individual well-being has made him a highly respected professional both in his home country and in his new community in Botswana.

Discover more of my works at:
https://books2read.com/asanchez

~~~